SPIRITUAL BOOTCAMP
THIS IS YOUR WAKE UP CALL

SPIRITUAL BOOTCAMP
THIS IS YOUR WAKE UP CALL

BY ROBERT PEASE

Spiritual Bootcamp: This is Your Wake Up Call

ISBN 978-0-9822019-0-9

Give It Wings Publishing Home
4909 E. McDowell Road
Phoenix, Arizona 85008
sales@robertpease.net
Website: www.robertpease.net
Cover Art Design by Sean McMahon

This book is dedicated
in Loving Memory of my
mother Jean Pease and sister Jan Goehring

It's all just one film to me. Just different chapters.
- Robert Altman

TABLE OF CONTENTS

CONTENTS

CONTENTS

As human beings, our greatness lies not so much in being able to remake the world as in being able to remake ourselves.

- Mahatma Gandhi

PREFACE

This book began as a collection of thoughts I downloaded into my mind as I was running on a treadmill at the gym. At first I wasn't clear why I was thinking about the ideas that are present in this book so I continued to run. When I run, my heart beats slower and my mind becomes clearer. Running is a form of meditation. Focused on my breathing and the rhythm of running I was opened to receive expanded ideas from within. I cannot say that I was listening at the time it took place but aware of the ideas flooding into my mind. After a few minutes the wave receded and I stepped off the treadmill to walk a few laps on the circuit to cool down.

I remember asking myself what will I do with all these thoughts and ideas? And I heard the reply, "You will write a book!" I remember immediately thinking, "Are you kidding me?" And the answer was, "No." I finished my workout and went into the shower to refresh in the cool water and once again heard a voice inside my head say, "Get ready for a new adventure!"

Over the next couple of weeks I thought deeply about what I would do with the information in my head. How would I form all the thoughts into a book? And as quickly as I asked the question I understood what I would do. I would teach a class on the information I had received. Now honestly, most people will say, "Just like that?" And I say, "Yes, just like that!" I have always known that when ideas are fresh in the mind it is important to act on them. The new thoughts are answers to the questions I ask and will guide me to the *one* creative thought required to create something new. I intuitively know the important part is to go into action and not doubt the information.

I decided it would be easier for me to teach a class and allow the information to be revealed as needed. I then realized I would teach a nine-week course and write each chapter before the class. I taught nine classes and wrote nine chapters. This was over two years ago and hundreds of people have taken the classes. I taught it like a college course for two hours a week! The class was accompanied by several books by authors that I believe held keys to furthering the information I was giving to the classes. So with nine weeks of classes and many books to read, I wondered whether anyone would take such a class. Especially one called Spiritual Bootcamp? But they came and grew along with me in the adventure and experiences we shared together. I realize that all this information is a lot to download, however, there is no time limit to growth.

Spiritual Bootcamp is more than a self-help book. It is a discovery of why we attract certain people and things to our lives. The foundation of this work is based on nine spiritual or natural principles that provide keys to awakening our journey to building within each of us a healthy, prospered and fulfilled life. By discovering how our natural talents empower others—to effectively increase their ability to enrich their lives—opens us to also receiving more value in our lives. For each of us, the keys to awakening are available in Spiritual Bootcamp to become fully aware of the attractors we are receiving from all our personal relationships. Understanding that the attractors are learning tools will allow us to expand in all areas and create true balance as both givers and receivers. The tools of empowerment offered in Spiritual Bootcamp are easy to apply to everyday life. We can begin today to transmute lack, unhappiness and sacrifice into total well-being by challenging ourselves to the greater understanding of life's purpose. Being ready and able is not enough! Ask yourself, "Am I now *willing* to have it all?"

This is a book filled with tools to guide all of us to understanding how important it is to fully receive. It took me a long time to open up to receiving. I thought it was all about giving. And like all of you, I gave until it hurt. I never thought that giving to myself was where it all begins. Giving to ourselves allows us to give more fully to others. I now understand that loving my life allows life to love me back. I know you will love learning how to receive fully as I and my students have learned to do the same. Being open and willing to fully receive is our life purpose.
Awaken with us and enjoy the complete journey!

Love and Light,
Robert Pease
Phoenix, Arizona

ACKNOWLEDGMENTS

First of all, I wish to acknowledge my students whose invaluable feedback over the last three years fed the process of this book. I wish to thank my clients who have continued to support this process in the creation. To my family and friends who have supported my journey throughout my entire life and imagined me to be more than I imagined myself. I wish to thank generously those folks who know me well and allow me to grow without condition. They are Dr. Tom and Lenita Pepper, my oldest friends of thirty years, Bill Harper, my closest companion who continues to make me laugh, Tom and Darlene Martinko, who offered me shelter while I wrote this book, Judith Manganiello, owner of A Peace of the Universe Bookstore in Scottsdale, AZ., who "held the space" for me and opened her arms so I could teach all my classes, give readings and express my joy everyday for three years, Elizabeth Allbee Da Silva, my right arm in business and my assistant Sarah Renshaw. I salute graciously and humbly my creative editorial compadres Suzy Jimerson-Overholt, Paige Sullivan, Jan Roelofs, Mary Dougherty, Jeffrey Peck, Crystal Lukens and Sean McMahon.

INTRODUCTION

As we move into the new millennium, it is a time of transformation into a new state of awareness. We have been busy on this planet making our way and learning to live together as One with a journey at times which has appeared to be arduous. It is time to stand up and pat ourselves on the back for having the courage to be here and do what is necessary to grow, for nothing ever is what it appears to be. We are learning that in order to have the world we want to create on the outside, we must first become the world we want to create on the inside.

This is truly the journey of the butterfly; firstly, we have been living lives voraciously absorbing everything in our paths to become saturated and full. Once filled with all that life has to offer, we begin to question whether we are happy as we are. For a moment we reflect inwardly to discover that there is more than we believe to be true. What parents, schools, governments and religions have tried in vane to interpret is now up to the individual to finally realize; that the possibilities are unlimited in the Universe.

What was once a voracious appetite towards life becomes a life not yet realized and unfulfilled as we grow older, and resignation oftentimes becomes the new habits of our limited imagination. But wait! Something begins to occur...CHANGE. Just as we begin to feel trapped by our fears and limited belief systems, the mind begins to search for a different journey. This change of growth in consciousness is due to new levels of awareness that create the shift we have been longing for in our lives. We have become aware of this present moment; the stillness has opened towards a new direction.

For many the stillness, or rather stuck-ness beckons the question, "I have arrived in the now, and now what?" The catalyst of change that has only been imagined beyond ourselves has led us to new avenues of thought. We are changing and growing into something extraordinary before our very eyes. We are opening our eyes to a new level of awareness that we haven't yet experienced!

INTRODUCTION

We are on the journey of the butterfly whether we know it or not. Through change we are in a state of metamorphosis because of all the thousands, or even millions of years of growth through evolution. Or more appropriately because of time and practice.

This book is a salute to the change which we are all a part of in this world. Spiritual Bootcamp is the journey of the butterfly and the challenge to all of us to make the changes necessary to enjoy the result of the voracious attempt by humanity to become more than we are today.

Everyone is born with talents and opportunities to make a difference in the world. Whether we are living in a hut or living in Manhattan, we are part of the great discovery within and our journey to understanding what we already know to be true… that we are a unique species and even more unique in our experiences. We are all told that we are alike and should do what we can do to survive. We are told that self-expression is only for the few, and that in order to make a difference we have to sacrifice more than what we have. This is baloney and it is being shoved down the throats by all the "dream stealers" who believe it impossible for themselves.

The truth is that we can discover within ourselves what we are here to fully understand in order to live happy, fulfilled, healthy and prosperous lives. We can map our consciousness by the aspects of ourselves that are always giving to others and by those parts of us that are here to receive from others. Unfortunately, we tend to be more a society of givers than receivers. We love empowering others more than we love empowering ourselves. And worse, given the opportunity, we will return most feelings of kindness faster than we will receive kindness within.

Through a step-by-step process, the journey of the butterfly is expressed within each chapter of this book. Each chapter focuses on where we are required to give of ourselves and where we are required to receive.

❖ Chapter One offers opportunities to develop the necessary skill set to utilize self-healing to balance our hectic lives while planting seeds of deliberate intention.

❖ Chapter Two opens our channels to being more intuitive and listen to our inner voice that is guiding us on our journey of self-discovery.

❖ Chapter Three will help each of us to empower our creative thinking to eliminate self-doubt and receive more clarity about what we truly want to create today.

❖ Chapter Four opens us to understanding that being practical, grounded and committed are the foundation for building an empowered life.

❖ Chapter Five gives us the opportunity to be open to trusting ourselves in order to attract more trust in our lives.

❖ Chapter Six taps into Self-love and how important it is to let go of the victims and the worrywarts in our lives, including the ones which live in our minds.

❖ Chapter Seven focuses on figuring out what is the real "work" we are experiencing through the process of understanding ourselves. We spend a great deal of our time asking life to show us what it is we are here to do, and then as soon as we discover what it is, we run in the opposite direction afraid we are unable to accept help from others.

❖ Chapter Eight asks the questions of what do we really think is important in life, self-respect and self-esteem or self-worth and self-sacrifice? Can we find the balance between being spiritual beings and the material things? The answer is "Yes!"

❖ Chapter Nine will help all of us to understand our roles as leaders, teachers and individuals by "getting off the roof" and becoming the role models for others. Once we have acknowledged ourselves as unique, we can then create what life's purpose is offering us—the journey of the butterfly as self-expression.

Spiritual Bootcamp is a course in life. Throughout this book we will understand what we can do to allow our lives to be joyful. We have it within each of to be truly happy once we let go of all the junk we have

INTRODUCTION

accumulated in our minds.

Each chapter of this book is filled with tools that will help us to make the right choices to develop balance between the giver and the receiver within and to express more discernment by knowing when to say yes and when to say no.

Spiritual Bootcamp originated as a nine-week course for students of spirituality. It has evolved into a book about guiding each of us to opening up to receiving more fully what we think we do not understand, but are required to know in order to be more fully aware. We have been programmed to believe we should do what we are best at and avoid that which we are lousy at doing. It is actually the opposite! What we are able to do well we will do anyway because those things come naturally and we naturally attract people to us who want to understand those aspects more fully for themselves. The things we do not do well create blocks and obstacles to creating what we want because we are unwilling to allow others who have these talents and abilities to teach us what they know naturally within. We push them away because we do not understand what they are willing to give to us. We do this because we are spending much of our time being busy giving to others or trying to figure out what will make them like us more and/or what will make us happier.

Through a series of discoveries at the end of each chapter we will exam why we are so unwilling to learn even though we think we are open-minded. We think this because we are limited by our habits, beliefs and our imagination.

Through affirmations we begin to affirm positive thoughts that allow us to become better receivers, which in turn will make us better givers no longer only willing to give what we think the other person needs. We begin to give to ourselves more fully and through the awareness of positive affirmed thoughts, the gifts of our true Self as Love.

Chapter 1

The Seed

The saying goes, "*There's no better place to start than at the beginning.*"

The first place to start is with the first person we know—our own, unique Self. I am the first person and the last person who is with me from the beginning to the end of my life! The record of my journey is recorded in the entirety of my personal experiences.

I am the maker of my own personal movie that portrays the saga of my life. I am the journey maker in this sense; and more importantly, this role places each one of us as the co-creator in collaboration with All That Is and the Divine Light Within.

"*Wait a minute,*" you say, "*are you talking about me?*"

Yes, I am. I am talking about all of us.

All that we ever are and all we will ever be is a personal creation in collaboration with the Universal Mind. We are manifesting everything in our lives. Each and every moment we are making our own movie with every thought we think, every wish we make and with every song in our heart we sing.

The question is, do we like the movie we are making?

Each day we have the perfect opportunity to wake up and ask these questions to our Self: Is my life being filled with joy? Am I open and allowing anything I desire to come true? The important word is *allowing*.

We have an opportunity to create only what allows us to feel good about our Self and the script we are developing depends on how we feel about what we think.

❖ **Do I feel that I am in alignment with my thoughts?**

If not, then today is another opportunity to create the movie I want to make. This is my opportunity to plant new seeds with deliberate intention to cultivate those seeds moment to moment, and have those seeds blossom into the realization of my highest desires. One of the greatest intentions is to feel good each day about the garden called *My Life* that I plant and cultivate to bountiful fruition.

The Art of Beginning

The word *beginning* is a powerful word filled with equally powerful intentions. It means a new starting place. In this place we embrace only to let go of the experiences of the past and allow new understanding to occur in our lives in order to become present today. The "understanding" is often misunderstood as forced change instead of willing growth. It is not necessary to believe in change for change's sake but to allow transformation to occur through understanding the relevance in what life is offering.

The art of beginning is knowing that everything is consciousness through growth and it can be easier if the path of transformation is understood from the journey so far.

The art of beginning takes courage we are often not aware of having within ourselves. Starting something new, choosing to create a new path on a journey and then resolving to take it step by step on an unknown road can be very scary. It takes courage to step out again and again, into the deeper adventure of knowing our Self and willingness to accept that loss and gain are equally balanced creating the transformation.

So the first thing we want to do is stand up and pat ourselves on the back for having the courage to be open and willing to grow through celebrating life and not in beating the Self up for it.

The art of beginning is the time when we say to our Self, *"I am allowing the abundance of my life to bring me everything I desire from a place of joy!"*

This new focus allows us to desire something more than what we usually allow ourselves. Here, we look to a future that is filled with all we are worthy of creating and are willing to receive from the understanding that we are already all we ever will create. The Who-I-Am asks, *"What is it that I now desire? Do my beliefs have value for myself and others and are they in alignment with my receiving value in return?"*

Asking these questions leads to more important questions like, *"How will I manifest that which gives me the treasure of feeling good?"* and *"When will I begin?"*

The real questions to ask are, *"Am I ready to receive without judgment of how it will come?"* and more importantly, *"Is what I desire in harmony with who I am?"*

The process of understanding and answering these questions will be clearer as we set our intentions and hold new beliefs even when we do not believe they are true; for example, believing I am prospered and buying anything I want, even when there is no money in the bank. Or believing I am attractive and loving, even when I do not think it is true.

The art of beginning is planting those first seeds, holding the intentions for growth of consciousness through change, visualizing the outcome in the blossoming and accepting it as if it has already happened. Every seed is planted with the intention that it will flourish.

4

It is planted not with expectation but with already knowing what the outcome will be.

In this book we will develop affirmations that can change the inner dialogues which allow us to heal ourselves. This will be the art of beginning and allowing us to walk on the road less chosen yet available to each and everyone.

Numbers and Symbols

Throughout this book I will be referring to numbers and symbols to connect concepts of energies and ideas together to form what I will discuss in Chapter Two as the Map of Manifestation. The importance of numbers and the physical aspects they hold are based on earlier ideas held by St. Augustine of Hippo (A.D. 354–430) who wrote, "Numbers are the Universal language offered by the deity to humans as confirmation of the truth." The single most important early philosopher to use numbers to be symbolically linked to physical manifestations was Pythagoras (6th Century). Regarded as the father of numbers was himself a holistic healer who believed everything has numerical relationships. It is up to the conscious Self to explore and investigate the secrets of these relationships or have them revealed by the Higher Self.

The idea of a *secret relationship* has led to the study and practice of understanding numbers in numerology, a study in the hidden meanings of numbers and their influence on human life. For the purposes in this book, I will be referring to numbers and using some of the ideas brought forth by numerologists but only to the extent explored in Chapter Two of this book.

I believe there is a connection between human design and sacred numbers as reflected in the idea of sacred geometry, which holds that geometry and mathematical ratios, harmonics and proportion are also found in music, light and cosmology.

In numerology the number one (1) represents the Self, it represents a multiplicative identity (tending or having the power to multiply) and it allows us to take a look at our Self as an individualized seed being. A seed being is a human who has the ability to create or multiply astronomically as much as can be infinitely imagined. However, in the sense that we are discussing here, the art of becoming, of discovering our Authentic Self, is the act of being creative and expanding into a deeper, more precious Self. As we set a course to knowing our Self on a more meaningful level than ever before, we may appear self-absorbed to others. What they may be really aware of is that we have the courage to step out of our comfort zone and show the willingness to grow in consciousness.

One is the only 1-perfect number.

One is the seed from which it is possible that all things can be created. One has the potential to express itself in infinitely possible ways. And One is the Divine wholeness and expression ultimately progressing in the potential of every *thing* in a unified field of consciousness.

Each chapter reflects this growth in consciousness from One to Nine and outlines how we can recognize what we are giving and what we are receiving in our Divine co-creative process. Developing a deeper understanding of what we do and how we reflect with each other will create a better understanding of why we attract and magnify certain behavior patterns that create resistance over and over again. More importantly, why out of the billions of people on the planet we attract certain types of people to us in our everyday life.

Affirmed Intentions

An intention is simply a resolution. It is from free will that we hold and resolve specific desires. Intentions arise from the choices we make from our ideas. The mind is where the ideas from infinite Source are manifested as thought *forms* or thought *things*. Thought forms are also known as Sacred Geometry. Meaning, as Source, or Infinite Light expresses it refracts—much as a crystal prism—into colors (both visible and invisible) which then further expresses into geometrical forms and manifests as all that we see. What we see is the sacred geometry we call Life. With our Self as co-creator, we collaborate with what we choose to believe both seen and unseen. Note the word *choose*!

However, if what we hold to be true is a set of thoughts, packaged as beliefs that are not in alignment with our desires, we become bogged down in the old system of dialogue. This inner dialogue causes us to struggle with how successful the outcome will be. Or worse, it causes us to fail.

When we desire to hold a new intention and plant the seed for further growth, we must first look at our inner dialogue. This is the voice inside us that may urge us forward into action or the voice that tells us we will have to get through our Dream Stealers first.

What are the Dream Stealers? They are any or all of the following: the inner dialogue in our mind, the voices from the past, the voices from our family, friends and co-workers, past and present, who beat down new intentions, dreams and desires. Most of us encounter our Dream Stealers early in life. Have you ever heard them say:

· *You will never be able to make a decent living if you don't get a college degree.*
· *It is okay to be creative, but only as a hobby.*

· *Make sure you marry someone who is financially secure.*
· *Don't tell them what you really feel, because you will not be liked.*
· *I had to settle for your father, and I am okay.*
· *What makes you think you can get that job with your background?*
· *Make sure you decide early what you want to do because it will be harder when you are older.*

❖ **What inner dialogues do you hear and still believe to be true?**

Something has been brewing inside of my mind for a while. There is something I wish to do, yet there is a discouraging voice inside me saying, *"Why do you want to do that?"* So instead of allowing the desire to grow, it is stifled! Every time I think about it, a feeling swells up inside of me creating a queasy and uncomfortable feeling. It causes me to be afraid of speaking my dream out loud. It is a fear of what someone else might say about my dream.

When we buy into the negative affirmed thoughts of Dream Stealers we *purchase* the desire unrealized by self-doubt, thus selling ourselves into becoming the Dream Stealers in return. The Dream Stealers are always here to remind us of why we must fail.

If we decide not to pursue our most cherished dreams, the Dream Stealers, stays in its comfort zone. The last thing a Dream Stealer wants is for anyone else to step out of him-or herself and challenge a new beginning. *If you can do it, why can't I?* This question can never be asked. The Dream Stealers needs to feel secure so no one else will ever become someone different than the person they see now. The Dream Stealers resist change and establish a firm hold on past experiences preferring to repeat rather than risk.

❧ ❧ ❧

The Dream Stealers will often be subtle. After you have shared your desire, they will smile and tell you how wonderful it sounds. They will tell you how excited they are for you and how lucky you are! But afterwards they will begin by saying:

· *Can you really afford it?*
· *What will your wife/husband say?*
· *How will you support yourself?*
· *I had a friend who tried that and they lost all their money.*
· *Don't you need more experience to do that?*
· *Are you sure that there is a need for that?*
· *It takes more talent than you think.*
· *But you already have a stable, secure job.*

❖ **What do Dream Stealers say to you?**

❧ ❧ ❧

In the mind of the Dream Stealers any success by others mirrors its failure. The Dream Stealer then has everything to gain when convincing us of our own lack of self-worth, self-esteem and self-love. Sometimes dreams are shattered and are never recovered, and negative affirmed thoughts of failure are reinforced by an unfriendly world. They fear our success will no longer require them to be present in our life and they will be abandoned.

The Dream Stealer does not understand that *no one is left behind!*

❖ **Am I a Dream Stealer?**
❖ **What inner dialogues can I change?**

· *I have to work hard for everything I get.*
· *Anything worth having never comes easily.*
· *I love to dance but my husband won't go dancing with me.*
· *I want to start my own business, but where will the money come from?*
· *I love my wife/husband, but I am no longer in love with her/him.*
· *If only I had finished school.*
· *I am too old to start over.*
· *Will I ever meet my soul mate?*
· *If only I were thinner, I could be happy.*
· *The last time I tried something new I didn't like it.*
· *I can't go out by myself; the city is too dangerous.*
· *I can't afford to go back to school.*
· *The harder I try, the worse it gets.*

What we believe to be true in the mind is true.

So how do we create new intentions without fear of each outcome? How do we create anything and know it will happen?

We create everything through deliberate intention for our best and highest good. The highest good simply means that which reflects wholeness from knowing we are already healthy, prosperous and fulfilled. A deliberate intention is a focused resolve to already be open and willing to grow.

How long does a rock hold an intention of being a rock? Millions of years!

How long do we hold a positive affirmed intention? Probably for a lot shorter time than we hold a negative one. We can hold the negative affirmed intention of "I hate my job" or "I am not happily married" longer than "I love myself" and "I am successful in my relationship."

We know how to repeat the negative affirmed intentions over and over again in our mind. It's easy, because we believe them to be true. We say negative affirmed intentions over and over again continuing to validate them as facts only to magnify the intentions to our Self every day. What we focus on is what we create.

❖ **What negative affirmed intentions do I hold onto?**

In the art of beginning, the intention is everything. If the intention has not been set originally for our highest and best good, in Divine Order, then anything can happen—meaning if we ask for something we think we desire and find out down the road it includes a journey we did not wish to take, we will then be resistant to it and the outcome can attach to many lessons along the way. That intention could also be connected to an inner Dream Stealer; i.e., *I have to work hard to get what I want.*

The same concept can apply when we are not connected to our receivership. This is simply when we desire things in life and are not fully open to receiving them. We stop the process for receiving along the way. We push them away because we do not feel worthy to accept them. For example, we can ask for more love in our lives and yet not allow it to flow into our lives. This arises from a lack of self-love and what will be attracted in turn will reflect this back mirroring and validating how we feel. Oftentimes we decide to judge the experience rather than be open and willing to accept love from all possibilities including the Self. To wit: *I want more love in my life only if I can also have it as a tall, dark and handsome stranger! I desire more love in my life, but not if I have to support them.*

As any new opportunity approaches we tend to deflect it with what we have experienced from past perception. For example: *My intention was to create this and something else showed up that I did not ask for. How can this be?*

The reality is that we probably didn't ask for what we required for our highest and best good. Or perhaps we settled for a little less than what we believed we deserved.

Connecting to our highest vibration through right action will give us what we deeply desire. Tapping into our deepest desires is in direct relationship to our deepest feelings. The deepest feelings act as the magnet. Unfortunately, most of the time our deepest feelings are layered below guilt, shame or frustration.

Guilt is tapped into and held in a negative affirmed intention without ever taking the deeper journey to discover how we can remove the past programming and begin to positively affirm with deliberate intention that the old stories are not who we are now. Again this idea asks to accept today as a new day without attachment to what the outcome will be based on old stories played over and over again in the subconscious mind programs. These are the programs that continue to attract and magnify what is no longer necessary to believe.

Being open and willing to grow is being open to a change in the field of consciousness and the field of new dreams.

When asking for anything, be quite sure it is a clear, deliberate, positive affirmed intention. State it for the highest and best good and in Divine Order. We might add "ease and grace" too! When our intentions are clear, we can be assured that what is not for our highest good will not be created; for once created it is often harder to correct it and the lessons may take us to places we wish we had not tread.

What we "focus on is what we create" becomes imagined, affirmed, positive intentions, which bring more happiness into our conscious field of living.

It is here that we are required to make sure the desired seeds we plant are sowed in grounded dialogue, allowing us to *already* know the growth is *fulfilled* in health, wealth, and prosperity.

Often the reason we decide not to ask for it at our highest spiritual vibration is because we do not *trust* the deeper meaning of our life. This is because we are disconnected from the collaboration and integration of our Spirit, Mind, and Body—the unified field of all consciousness.

The disconnected Self embraces all it has already experienced, thinking it understands the journey so far and hopes it will work out in the end, instead of understanding there are deeper resources at work in an abundant universe, outside the visible range of what we can hear, taste, smell, touch and see. The universe is made up of both seen and unseen. It is possible to know there is more, yet not really believe it, while forgetting our future vision is connected to yet another great "sense." An unseen sense that echoes in nature, "I AM THAT I AM" and am already complete in the creation what we are in the mind of the universe.

❖ **What positive affirmed deliberate intentions am I trusting for my "highest and best good and in Divine Order"?**

Vibrations

Colors, numbers, words, animate, inanimate and most importantly, feelings are the vibrations of our lives. In this world today we are connecting with a greater understanding of vibrational energy and how it is who we are as Source. We are learning that what we feel is directly related to what we create. For so long as the notion of emotions was set on the back burner of our reality, we believed the thinking personal mind and the intelligence connected with it were vibrating at a higher level than our emotions The emotions were somehow only connected with our lower or animal Self and lastly, that they needed to be suppressed. Times have dramatically changed, as we now know, through the use of technology in science, we are connected to myriads of vibrations that demonstrate the multi-faceted vibrational universe we can see and the vibrational universe we cannot see. Everything is connected, everything is energetic, and there is no space in-between. The old Newtonian reasoning theorized that there is space between objects and only when things come into contact with each other is there change. Quantum science suggests there is a unified field of eternally connected consciousness affected by our perception, an inter-relationship of all dimensions, or Consciousness—consciously aware of Self as consciousness. There is no such thing as space in the universe but only cause creating effect as a pebble on water *ripples to the shore.*

Through vibrational sounds in the form of words, we connect to our inner world of un-manifest, or least obvious. From the ancient knowledge of Sanskrit, an ancient Indic language that is the language of Hinduism and the Vedas and is the classical literary language of India the *mantra*, an energy-based sound, creates thought energy waves which resonate inwardly to the Source of our beingness, or happiness. The use of mantras, or energy-based sounds accumulate over time connecting the conscious mind to the Universal Mind allowing a greater bond to be created and more conscious awareness of a state of happiness. Spiritually based mantras vibrate to magnify an effect overriding other smaller vibra-tions absorbing them and producing a new state of consciousness in tune with the spiritual energy connected to the mantra.

We know singing creates joy or distress in the singer and listener, and through our daily actions we are aware that words are sound vibrations that create both the obvious and the non-obvious in our life. Through words and their individual vibrational connections we reap what we sow. We call this cause and effect or karmic causation. What is energetically transmuted will create and reflect back to the cause to reveal what value it has in creation.

From ancient to present times we have used affirmations in the form of prayers to ask for blessings and to send and receive gifts for others and ourselves. We repeat prayers over and over again to create something from what seems to be from nothing. Words like actions are how we build beliefs that form our personal identity. We collect them out of the un-manifest, our source of being (*the Be-er*), and we think of them over and over again until we materialize whatever we desire by walking in the direction of our prayer through faith (action) as the *Do-er*.

Words, and what we think of them, connect us directly to another vibrational sonata—our feelings—the vibrational energy field where everything we desire we attract, whether we think we asked for it or not. Feelings are the responses we emanate from our emotional response center of our heart-mind. The power of feelings connecting to the universe will respond as the natural/spiritual laws that govern our relationship to the Higher Self. The laws are the instructions for guiding the growth of awareness in the unified field of consciousness.

What is important to understand is that what we feel is what we ultimately create in our lives by magnifying it to us. How we feel is what we magnetically attract, and what we feel becomes our daily bread, our manna as answered prayers. The universe does not judge the quality of the action instead it provides what is focused on by the creator of the feelings.

Understanding the importance of being aware of how we are feeling at every moment is at the heart of holding positive affirmed deliberate intentions. It is even more important to be conscious and aware that we are always feeling, even when we are busy in the personal mind *thinking*.

The mind appears to be attributed often to the brain. But when we ask our Self, "Where is my mind located?" the knowingness of who I AM answers, "Everywhere and nowhere." Perhaps it is time to understand that the mind dwells in the wholeness of who we are and therefore is in everywhere in the body an nowhere in Spirit.

In the personal thinking-mind we may be *thinking* we feel a certain way, yet in the heart-mind we may be feeling a different way, and both will reflect in our body-mind as a disturbance or dis-ease if we are not in accord and in balance.

· *I want a new car. (Thinking-mind) I don't deserve a new car. (Heart-mind) I am constipated. (Body-mind)*
· *I want a divorce. (Thinking-mind) I love my spouse. (Heart-mind) I cannot sleep soundly. (Body-mind)*
· *I need my job. (Thinking-mind) I hate my job. (Heart-mind) I have ulcers. (Body-mind)*

If we are not cooperating with our Self, then how can we ask the universe to reflect anything more back?

Visualizing the Outcome Without Expectations

As our inner dialogues are recognized as resonating with our intentions, we will benefit by being in the flow of our lives, without resistance and from the place of joy. The quiet flowing nature of holding our highest intentions will feel good. This kind of "feeling good" is love and love is peace. When we are peaceful, we are aware we are creating our perfect journey through conscious awareness.

Recognizing what our inner dialogues are saying is about listening to what we are thinking and speaking. *Do my thoughts and words feel good? Do they speak to myself of how perfect my life can be at any given moment? Do I feel good? Do my thoughts and words have value to others and to myself?* Knowing how we feel is becoming quiet in the stillness of the inner Self and feeling the feelings. It is the intuitive nature of inner workings of the Spirit.

There are many reasons why we do not feel good, or so we believe. If the time is taken to listen to the deeper feelings that are running on a current below our guilt, we will hear our true heart's desire speaking to us. Sometimes the reason it so difficult to be still and listen is we do not wish to face how we really feel about who we are married to, or how we feel about our current job or why we are at the place where we are in our present life-movie.

Taking this journey becomes difficult because in taking a deeper look at the inner Self, we have to acknowledge that what we are truly feeling may lead to change and major growth in how we are living our life. Facing what we really want, we may not be able to continue with what we have already created.

By examining our deeper feelings we can begin to connect with our *authenticity*. What this means will be discussed many times in the course of this book. For now, it is only important to begin to understand that we can connect with the Who-I-Am by sitting still and listening to the inner voice.

One of the many paths we will take is through visualizing the outcome without attaching any feelings to an expectation of the outcome.

There are many opportunities to feel good. All we need to know is that we can feel good anywhere and at anytime. And feeling good is synonymous with feeling peace, gratitude through appreciation, healthy and fulfilled.

၆ ၆ ၆

Imagine you are wishing to create a new career in a field that has held your interest and desire for many years. Now remember why you wanted to create it. Embrace how you feel every time you think about the new path. Remember why you feel good when you think about the new career.

၆ ၆ ၆

· *I have always wanted to own my own business.*
· *My best friend loved the idea of my being self-employed.*
· *I love to be with customers.*
· *I love to bake.*
· *I have dreamed of what the storefront looks like for years.*
· *I am a wonderful caregiver.*

When we visualize something there will be a feeling attached to the images in our mind. It is important to change the feelings of attachment to the peaceful feelings about what it is and already have created. It is all about how we feel about it that mirrors whether or not it is something we truly desire through the actions we are taking to prove it is true.

Remembering is the first key to understanding visualizations, and it is easy.

၆ ၆ ၆

When remembering anything it is connected with a feeling. Observe the feeling and decide whether it feels good or feels bad. Is it happiness or sadness? When the feeling is good, write it down on a sheet of paper.

· *Is it a place?*
· *A loved one's laughter?*
· *A new bicycle?*
· *A cruise to the Bahamas?*
· *A romantic date?*
· *A daughter's wedding?*
· *A puppy on a birthday?*
· *An "A" on a test?*
· *A lover's embrace?*

After writing down the moments, let them begin to play in the mind's eye. The mind's eye is commonly called the "third eye". The "third eye" is located just above and center of your eyebrows. Close your eyes and place your focus inward to your "third eye". Feel the feeling of *feeling good*, and then feel the feelings in your heart.

Next, connect these feelings to abundant health, infinite prosperity, a loving relationship, or home. Imagine yourself five years from now the way you wish to be in this new _____. See the location of the _____, how it looks, and smells, adding whatever details come to mind. Then in your mind's eye go to a mirror and see yourself in the mirror—how healthy and glowing you are in your reflection, how successful you are in your _____, and how glad you are you decided to take the leap of faith creating what it is you want. Now ask yourself to feel this way now. Say or think, " I am fulfilled in this place and time right now, immediately and eternally." Remember that only time and space separate you from the future and there is no time and no space in Truth. Now bring the feelings backwards in time to yourself at this very moment. Hold the feelings in your heart and mind and breathe. Know that you are

"All I Am." Sense that the heart and ALL I AM are unified. This is a visualization to remember without expectation of an outcome. The expectation is replaced with a sense of knowing all is well at this moment in your universe.

❖ **Visualize a time when you either experienced a tremendous
  healing or a tremendous revelation in your life. Focus on
  the event that brought you a peaceful clear mind and a sense
  of wonder and excitement in the healing or revelation.
  Visualize yourself feeling good, peaceful, healthy and fulfilled.**

৯ ৯ ৯

Now let us understand why we just created abundant health, infinite prosperity, a loving relationship, or home the way we did. There are many reasons why we could have decided not to make it a positive feeling. We could have decided we could not have connected with the *joy* of it because the life-movie so far reinforces the past.

· *I will never have enough money to open my own business.*
· *I don't have the experience to be self-employed.*
· *What if it fails and I lose all my savings?*
· *I will work long hours and never have any time off for myself.*
· *I tried a business before and lost everything.*
· *What if it fails and my family is disappointed?*
· *Marriages fail everyday.*
· *My doctor tells me I will never recover completely.*
· *I am dependent on my spouse.*
· *Where will the money come from for a new home?*

❖ **Make a list of the negative reasons for situations not working out the way you planned? Examine the script to see what changes need to be made to begin to imagine a different point of view.**

Every time we think about why we cannot have what we most desire, we create the inevitable outcome of it not being created. How we feel about what we want is what we will always have in the end because we felt the same way in the beginning made clear in the statement, "This is the beginning of the end!"

If we can hold the intention that is keeping us connected to the negative outcome and understand that it is the very reason we still do not have it, then how would it work if we held the opposite intention of that outcome and believed that we could have it? If an intention can work one way, why not in reverse? This is called a trick of the mind. Tricking our mind not to connect with our Dream Stealers but to connect with our true heart-felt desire is simple because the mind does not know the difference between what is real and what is symbolic. The mind is only for ideas to be sent to the subconscious to magnify what we want to attract!

The next thing to do is to believe that whatever the outcome will be, it will be for the best and highest good and in Divine Order, and that the abundant universe wants nothing less than to give us everything we truly desire. Every time we connect with the feelings that allow us to feel good, peaceful, healthy and fulfilled we disconnect with why we might fail.

The important opportunity is to believe in something that has not yet happened but will if we focus on the intention as if it has *already* happened. The trick is to continually feed the good feelings about having your own business, home, loving relationship or whatever you desire by remembering the feelings that allow you to feel good right now. It does not matter that the memories are not connected directly to your new desire. What matters is whether or not you are connecting the happy, joyful and good feelings everyday with what you wish to create. You begin to attract all that is feeling good into your universe and with it comes the feeling you can do whatever your heart desires because it comes from a place of joyfulness, playfulness and fulfillment.

❖ **What are some things that allow you to feel good? How often in the day do you think about them?**

Many times when we begin to create what we want we will also attach to how we want it to happen. This process removes the understanding that most of the time nothing happens the way we think it should. There is an innate part of us believing we must be in control of every aspect because we will be looked upon as incompetent if we leave it to chance. Control is *will* resisting openness and willingness to allow every possible opportunity to manifest. Resisting is to exert force for the opposition.

As soon as we begin to create what we think we desire, we simultaneously create the opposite of what we think we desire. The opposition creates the struggle and the struggle makes it hard work. When the frustration mounts up we begin to connect with why our creation will never be created, and then we become our own best Dream Stealer. When we begin to realize how the process works it becomes a game that we can change not through control but with positive affirmed thinking and feeling. Remember, we are making a movie called *My Life and How to Live It!* And we are making it up as we evolve!

Germinating Your Soul's Desire

A desire is a request. It is a longing for something. It is a feeling.

When we desire something we are wishing for it to become a reality. If we hold the desire long enough, it will be created. Oftentimes the desire is an illusion because we settle for less than the whole. We do this because we do not believe we can have the whole thing. We are afraid if we ask for the moon, it will be burdened with things we do not want.

The feeling of only deserving half the desire or the expectation we will not really get it, ultimately is our connection to our lack. It is saying to the Abundant Universe, "I really cannot allow it to come to me." We push it away with our will. The emotions of desire can attach to the feelings of loss, betrayal and abandonment. It triggers the opposite of what we think we are asking for in the beginning. Eventually we learn not to desire very much of anything and settle for what we are dished out. "Having it all" becomes a dialogue of "something is better than nothing."

· *I desired a boyfriend and I got a man just like my ex-husband.*
· *I desired an income raise and was let go of my job.*
· *I desired a kitten and it died.*
· *I desired more money and then had to work like a slave.*
· *I desired love and it brought more misery.*

❖ **What have you desired that manifested as lack?**

A desire for something will always create change. Oftentimes the change comes from mistakes. Mistakes have a negative connotation to many people. Mistakes are often seen as failures in the short term but later realized as successes in the long term. Mistakes are simply change to create growth in consciousness. It is our asking for something more than we already have at the moment. A desire can manifest from boredom, loneliness, frustration, anxiety, and anger. A desire is asking for change.

· *I am tired of being sick and tired.*
· *If only my girlfriend would get a job.*
· *I could do better if I wasn't micromanaged every day.*
· *I will be happier if only I have more money.*
· *I wish they would just leave me alone.*

If we are feeling distress when we wish for something and then we manifest it, why are we then even more distressed when we get what we asked for?

It is the feeling attached to the desire that will determine what we receive! Every day we are connecting feelings to desires and every day we are receiving what we may have desired from our past yesterdays, a past we only think we remember. However, the universe does remember and gives us exactly what we previously asked for and now don't remember what it was.

How important is it to know at every moment how we feel and what we desire?

Our best desires will manifest in the highest vibration when we know how we feel about something before we ask for it. The saying goes, *Think before you act.* A better saying is, **Feel before you think!**

Attaching a feeling with something, anything, can be created through conscious living and deliberate intentions. Being aware of the seeds we plant before planting them into our desires and emotional system will give us the understanding of what we can expect.

A great example is: When was the last time you set the intention for more awareness? A greater connection with the higher consciousness within? More compassion or better yet more patience?

Ultimately we will all begin to understand the only thing to hold an intention on is not a thing at all but something deeper. Begin holding the intention of life already being prosperous, healthy and fulfilled. If we are going to ask for what we finally want in the long run it is simply to have led a life that ends in the Soul having had a human experience and discovered what Higher Consciousness already is *Realized!*

Figure Out What You Desire

How can I be sure that what I have asked for I have asked for correctly?

Before asking for some thing we should ask, "How do I really feel about it?" When it is still an idea take a look at it without any attachment to the idea. Say, "I am taking a good look at it first before making any resolution regarding it."

ॐ ॐ ॐ

One way to look at the "something" is to make a list in two columns. The first column is called "Feel Good Memories" and the other column is called "Possible Desires."

❖ **In the first column list the memories that make you feel good. They do not need to be complete memories but only the parts that really allow you to remember how good you felt at the time. (It is the ability to time-travel that allows us to connect to** other times and places).

❖ In the second column list the things you want to create. Make them as specific as you can.

❖ When the two columns are complete, read the list of feel-good memories. Think about them for a moment making sure the list is only filled with thoughts that are *positive emotionally affirmed feelings*. If there are any that are not, scratch them off of the first column.

❖ Once the list is completed, sit in a quiet state or light meditation and think of the moments you were truly happy. Once the feeling of happiness is contained within, place the list inside the field of happiness, or the "light." When you are in a perfect state of feeling good, enjoy the feeling for a moment. Remember how wonderful it is to feel this good! Breathe the feeling in and out throughout the entire body.

❖ Now take a look at the second list of the things you think you want to have in the future. Go down the list one at a time and see if your *present* feelings are resonating with your *future* manifestation. When you read one that feels good, check it off. When you read one that does not feel good, simply mark through it. This is very close to following a "hunch" or a "gut feeling."

❖ When you have completed the list make another list with only the wishes you checked off in the second column. Once you have done this take a look at them as one desire and imagine them in a bright white ball in your mind's eye.

❖ Look once again at the list of memories and magnify your

feelings to a bigger bright white ball and then surround your wish list, entwining the two into one single ball of bright white light. With your eyes closed and a smile on your face, simply and quietly feel good. And then let the ball go! Say to yourself, "Give it wings!"

You are now <u>feeling</u> before you are <u>thinking</u> about your desires. Then say to yourself, ***"For my best and highest good and in Divine Order!"***

With practice you will begin to do this all the time. You will know that what it is you desire has already manifested, and you feel good even before you see it because it is already here and now. Giving it wings and letting it go suggest to the mind symbolically that it has already been created.

Making A List-Checking It Twice

Another opportunity for creating a desirable, deliberate intention is making a treasure map. They are fun and done with the same joy as the exercise above. Treasure mapping is not a magic pill but another opportunity to focus on what we want to create. All types of visualization techniques are symbolic representations of what we desire and are not tools of some occult practices but simply tools of magical thinking. When we map our desires on paper we are creating a navigational system to help us remember what the vision looks like and that we gave it wings! Treasure mapping is reminding us to appreciate the abundant universe and that life is a gift.

Ꮐ Ꮐ Ꮐ

There are many kinds of treasure maps. Like the "feel good" list you created from the last section in this book, once again list all things you want to create today. Make sure the list only includes feel good ideas. Buy a beautiful box, or make one! Place the pieces of papers inside this box. The important thing is to feel happy and joyful while creating the box and while placing the papers inside.

After the box is filled and closed tightly say out loud, *"This treasure box is filled with joy and happiness. So be it! And so it is!"*

Place the box in the favorite part of your home where you can see it every day. You can add new wishes whenever you want. But make sure they are things you truly desire and bring feelings of joy. Every month open the box and take out the ones that have manifested and look at the ones that have yet to be revealed to the naked eye. Remember why you placed them in the box and then close the box and open it again next month. You will be surprised how quickly the box will empty!

I suggest that you begin by placing feelings in the box. Remember *things* will always be present in our world because we are creating them and buying them faster than we can build garages to store them. Life has much to offer besides just being the land of more. Ask for the nature of the universe to reveal the special gifts. Write words on pieces of paper. Words like:

· *Desires Fulfilled!*
· *Higher Consciousness!*
· *Abundant Health!*
· *Immediate Happiness!*
· *Loving Unity With My Family!*
· *Playfulness!*

- *Infinite Prosperity!*
- *Loving Friendships!*
- *Balanced Relationships!*
- *Love! Love! Love!*

§ § §

The next successful opportunity is to tap into your inner child and get out the arts and crafts box. This visualization tool is to take a large poster board in your favorite color and begin placing pictures and words that bring you the same joy from your wish list. Affix stars and shiny, glittering trim to the poster. Do not hesitate to fill up the board with all kinds of feel-good wishes. Once the poster board is filled, take a piece of string or rope and glue it around the edge of the board making sure you have enough to close the two ends. Just before you seal the rope or trim, imagine your feel good thoughts. Feel peaceful, healthy and prosperous and then glue the ends together, blowing a kiss as you do, so that your treasure map is sealed with a kiss! Then give it wings! Place the poster board on your kitchen pantry door where you can see it every day. Whenever you look at the board simply feel good about what you see. Remember, what you focus on is what you create!

Co-creating With Our Higher Self

The universe is infinite possibilities. We are a universe unto ourselves.

It has been suggested that the "kingdom of Heaven is within." I am suggesting that the Universe of All Happiness is within.

In the art of beginning it is possible to understand a simple new belief, a new collection of thoughts. Imagine the universe in its abundance and the only thing it wants is to give us everything we ask for, without prejudice and without any personal attachment. The universe is here for the asking and all we need do is ask. Well, it is not ALL we need to do, but more about that later! Think of the universe as the divine all-having, all-knowing and all-giving. Think of yourself as the receptacle to all that it has to offer. In your mind begin to know this as a new feeling, the feeling of unconditional transparent abundance for your best and highest good. Knowing and accepting that we are already willing and open to receive all that we may allow in the name of joy.

· *In the infinite wisdom, feel safe. I am always safe!*
· *In the depth of the heart, know love. I am love!*
· *In the body, know health and wellness. I am already healthy and wealthy!*

ॐ ॐ ॐ

All THERE IS is ALL-I-AM but in the personal mind all I am is what I believe to be true and also false. If my beliefs are not allowing me to feel good about myself, that is, happy, healthy and fulfilled, then it is time to rethink who I *really* AM. *This is my new journey. This is my new intention.* More importantly, who I think I am is the message I send to my subconscious and then becomes manifested in my biology. My beliefs are expressed in who I see when I look in the mirror—the biological person standing before myself.

ॐ ॐ ॐ

In a universe of infinite possibilities we stand at the leading edge of all that ever will be. In the infinite wisdom of the universe, we are the divine abundance expressing through Self as who we are right now. We are co-creating with the universe as unique expressions of all that already IS. In our individual, unique adventure we are experiencing infinite possibilities to share with each other forever. The infinite universe is joy, peace and love. We are experiencing the unique journey that will lead us back to the very joy, peace and love we know we already are. We are at home in the universe, and everything is exactly the way it is meant to be at this moment in the singular possibility expressed in being human. Everything is perfect in the universe. We are perfect expressions on infinite journeys into the perfect adventures we are sharing with each other and everything animate and inanimate in life.

When we finally connect to this we know the only things truly worth having are joy, peace and love in every intention we create! Together we are co-creating it all.

Universal Life Force

The old saying goes, *"You'll be led to and given what you need at the right time on your journey without knowing it."*

Energy is always emanating from the physical bodies of all beings. Reiki is a gift of the universe that *everyone* can tap into and use in their daily lives.

What is Reiki? Reiki (pronounced Ray-key) is a Japanese word meaning "Rei" (universal, cosmic life force) and "ki" (the flowing life-force that binds everything). It is believed to have originated in Tibet and then reintroduced again by a Japanese man named Dr. Usui Mikao. Hence, the Japanese word, Reiki.

Whatever the name and from wherever it came, the one important thing about Reiki is that it is for everyone, regardless of personal religious choices and beliefs. Reiki is about connecting to the power of the abundant universe and channeling the pure universal life force through each of us for the extraordinary effects it has on our lives for the better!

Through a process of initiations, the dormant Reiki energy becomes accessible. It is possible then to use the energy to heal everything animate and inanimate. The word healing in this case means having the ability to bring into balance, peace and awareness anything that is in discord or dis-ease.

There are many books written about Reiki and the effects generated from the use of the universal life force. There are also many books written concerning the use of hands-on healing practiced throughout the world by Divine Light workers, energy workers, healers and those proficient in channeling.

This book is not going to cover the story of Reiki. For that information you will be directed to a website offering you valuable information and reference material to enhance and master Reiki symbols and attunements. Also for further understanding it is easy enough to simply use a search engine on the Internet to discover a multitude of books, lectures, teachers and studies, both clinical and spiritual.

My intention is to simply offer everyone the opportunity to connect with types of Reiki you can use during your growth and development while studying from this book. I believe it is important to connect with at least one healing modality that we can use every day. This is the energy technique I have chosen for you to use during your work with this book. If you already have other modalities you are using, Reiki can be applied without any reservation to what you are now practicing. It is harmless, effective, effortless and cumulative in much the same way as meditation. All the energy we require at any given time is all we will receive.

In order to receive the Reiki attunements, you will be required to go to a website which will offer you the information necessary to become attuned. This process is free to you and anyone else you know who is looking for avenues of healing. I offer free Reiki attunements in my workshops as part of the exploration and growth of my students. Normally during the Spiritual Bootcamp seminars the students are attuned to three levels of Reiki over a period of nine weeks. However, for those of you unable to attend my workshops and seminars, I offer the opportunity to become attuned to all three levels at one time! This will be a wonderful healing experience for you and your personal community. Remember that the pebble on the water ripples out infinitely.

The attunements you will receive will encourage further growth to higher consciousness with ease and grace. Self-healing is a gift that keeps giving and will further help you in becoming a better receiver.

So much of our time is wishing to be of service to others however, in order to facilitate the highest level of giving; we need to be able to receive in return. There is balance in the universe that creates cooperation in the nature of each and every one of us. Remember, receivership is ours for the *allowing*.

Please take the time to visit my website at **www.reikivibes. net**. The website will give you more information regarding Reiki and the powerful healing tools that will enhance your daily life. After you are attuned you will receive an email giving you the date and time you have received Reiki attunements.

Diagrams showing you how to do the Universal Life Force healing will also be available for you. If you are further interested in studying at a deeper level, receiving certifications, teaching Reiki and studying other forms of Reiki

Healing you may wish to purchase my instructional Reiki Master manual. There are no requirements to purchase the Reiki manual to be able to simply use self-healing. Going to the website and filling out the form is all that is required to become a practitioner of Reiki and receive all the benefits for self-healing and guiding others to heal themselves.

If you choose to begin practicing Reiki, I suggest it become part of your daily meditation. I apply Reiki daily, usually in the morning and before I go to sleep. However, you are able to apply Reiki anytime when convenient for you. The important thing is to make it part of your day, especially while reading and studying Spiritual Bootcamp.

For further information and attunements please go to **www.reikivibes.net**.

Discovery

1. Do you feel you are in alignment with your thoughts? Explain what this means.

2. What dialogues did you hear and still believe to be true?

3. What do your Dream Stealers say to you?

4. Are you a Dream Stealer? Make a list of things you say to yourself blocking you from moving in the direction of your prayers.

5. What is your inner dialogue? (Example: I always have to work hard for everything!)

6. What intentions do you focus on?

7. What intentions are you asking for that reflect your highest and best good and in Divine Order?

8. Visualize a time or event when you either experienced a tremendous healing or a tremendous revelation in your life. Focus on this event that brought you a peaceful clear mind and a sense of wonder and excitement in the healing or revelation. Visualize yourself feeling good, peaceful, healthy and fulfilled.

9. Make a list of the negative reasons for situations not working out the way you planned? Examine the script to see what changes need to be made to begin to imagine a different point of view.

10. What are some things that allow you to feel good? How often in a day do you think about them?

11. What have you desired that manifested as "lack?"

12. List the memories that make you feel good. They do not need to be complete memories but only the parts that really allow you to remember how good you felt at the time. It is the ability to time-travel that allows us to connect to other times and places.

13. Now list the things you want to create. Make them as specific as you can.

14. When the lists are completed, read the list of feel-good memories. Think about them for a moment making sure that the list is only filled with thoughts that are positive emotional feelings. If there are any that are not, scratch them off of your first column.

15. Once the list is completed, begin invoking the memories in your mind and connect them into a ball of energy of the feelings the fond memories will bring up. When you are in a perfect state of feeling good, enjoy the feeling for a moment. Remember how wonderful it is to feel this good! Know you can feel happiness whenever you want.

16. Now take a look at the second list of the things you think you want to have in the future. Go down the list one at a time and see if your present feelings are resonating with your future wishes. When you read one that does feel good, check it off. When you

read one that does not feel good, simply mark through it.

17. When you have completed the list make another list with only the wishes you checked off in the second column. Once you have done this take a look at them as one desire and imagine them in a ball of light in your mind's eye.

Look once again at the list of memories and magnify your feelings to a bigger ball and then surround your wish list, entwining the two into one single ball. With your eyes closed and a smile on your face, simply and quietly feel good.

18. Option 1: Make a treasure map. Place all the pictures and words that describe the above list you have created. All of these items, thoughts and pictures feel good. They represent your deliberate intentions so be sure to "give it wings!" Be creative! Use an assortment of colored papers, metallic stars, and bright markers. Be sure to place the treasure map in a place where you will see it everyday. The kitchen is a great place! Include others in your household in creating treasure maps.

19. Option 2: Make a treasure box or use one you love and then fill it with small pieces of paper (I like mixing colors!) with the affirmations you wish to enhance in your life. Examples are to write down words like "Abundant Health!" "Infinite Prosperity!" "Loving Relationships!"

20. Have fun with this process. In your imagination believe everything on the map or in the treasure box has already come true!

21. Practice Reiki everyday. It is great to wake up in the morning

a little bit earlier and continue laying in bed placing your hands on the locations described on the Reiki website. Practice 15-30 minutes everyday or as often as you can allow yourself. This practice evolves just like meditation. The more you practice the better you will feel. Remember, it is not important whether you believe it is working, it is only important that you do it. It is important that you hold the intention of being healthy, prosperous and fulfilled. Enjoy, relax and be still.

The only real valuable thing is intuition.
- Albert Einstein

Chapter 2

Cooperation is Balance

What is temperance? Is it something we understand because we are in the flow of our experience through change, flexibility, and because we are relaxed in our daily lives? Or is it something we are struggling with constantly because we are not in moderation in our actions, thoughts or feelings?

Balance is often a major issue in life. It is often found in struggling between giving more than we are receiving, whether to say "yes" or say "no," offering too much help or none at all. Even more importantly, it is found in understanding when to allow others to take responsibility and then being able to let go of the need to be responsible for their actions, thoughts and feelings.

How much time do we spend over-cooperating with others? Or under-cooperating with others because of feeling over-burdened with responsibilities?

Even more importantly, how much time do we spend with the constant challenge of connecting between a balance of "what I feel and what I think?" Especially when we know we are spending too much time in thinking-mind or the opposite, too much time in the heart-mind!

In order to achieve a certain balance and achieve cooperation we need to understand first the internal conflicts related to discord. "Am I being a worrywart on the mental plane, or overly reacting to what I am feeling emotionally? Do I need to be responsible to everybody, including myself, even when I do not feel like it?"

I call this being the *hall monitor*. In elementary schools someone is always given the responsibility of being the hall monitor. They get to wear a plastic badge designed like a shield whenever it is their turn to walk the halls to make sure everyone in the hall has a pass. If anyone appears to be roaming freely, then the hall monitor is to take him or her to the principal's office for further interrogation. The hall monitor then returns to the job at hand, making sure the hallways are being supervised.

A couple was spending the weekend at home doing tasks they both felt they needed to do to keep their lives in order. The husband was busy in the garage sorting through all the boxes that had been stacking up on the sidewall for months. He decided to go through them and clear them out. The wife was busy in the bedroom painting a wall that she had wanted to be a different color for years. Both were doing their respective duties. In an interim the wife took a break and decided to see what her husband was doing in the garage. She discovered him busy in the boxes. She decided to start taking a closer look at what he might be throwing away and to make sure there was nothing in the boxes she wanted to keep. She had a deep desire to be involved in what he was doing instead of continuing along her path of painting the room. She needed to take over some of the responsibility he had chosen because she thought he would not do the job to her liking. Part of her just knew she could do a better job! As long as he was only reorganizing the boxes she felt it would be okay, but now she was afraid after he finished she would not be able to find anything again.

Busying herself with his work perturbed the husband and he began feeling she was micro-managing his affairs. They began to argue and he dropped what he was doing and left the garage telling her if she could do a better job, then she should do it herself!

Only trying to help she was frustrated by his lack of understanding, she stormed back into the bedroom to continue painting. Upset she began to think about how ungrateful her husband could be and the only reason she had been painting the bedroom was because she had asked him to do it in the past and he had never gotten around to it.

Hall monitors need to make sure everyone else is doing everything "the right way"! Hall monitors believe they are here to *fix* everyone else's mistakes or to make sure others do not do it "wrong" in the first place.

The hall monitor lives in all of us at sometime. The need to fix everybody else can become the focus of an entire life path if it is not corrected through awareness.

As a "healer" I never understood how I could help anyone else heal since I was dysfunctional myself. I kept feeling there must be a lot more to what I thought I was doing but could not quite put my thoughts in the right perspective. I became distressed with feeling unworthy of allowing the universe to apply any wisdom through me and I felt like a fraud!

What I eventually began to realize through sharing with others my healing work was a very simple but a huge aha! I am not here to heal anyone but myself. Once I felt the peace that comes with revelation I then started merrily going about my business of simply sharing with others what I understood. Eventually the sharing led to understanding a deeper core issue in myself which swelled up from my deeper emotional programs. I realized through my healing practice that part of the reason for working in a healing modality was to enlighten me in understanding my deep need to fix people. Some part of my inner beliefs spiraled around constantly needing to give until they got it. *Got what?* Well what I thought needed fixing! Never mind whether they were asking for help or not.

My self-healing was beginning to allow me to take a look at the deeper core issues of why I thought and acted in a certain manner, and what this need to fix was all about.

In college I felt a need to excel in everything I was doing. I wanted to be an exemplary student and make straight A's. The reason for this was partly due to my lack of formal education. I had only gone to the seventh grade before dropping out of school and going to work. So my need to be accepted by my peers propelled me into a need to be the best so I could prove myself and be honored for my abilities.

One day in class I was standing in front of the assembly reading a speech I had written for the class assignment. About half way back in the classroom two girls were talking and giggling with each other. I became overwhelmed with a need to know why they were talking and more importantly were they giggling and talking about me? I became so frustrated with them—even though no one else was probably aware of them—I tossed my speech at them and stormed out of the classroom.

About half way down the corridor the Professor caught up with me, grabbing my arm to stop me and suggested firmly that I should stop by his office after my classes. Still upset I marched on through the corridor.

Later in my meeting with him he sat smiling at me from across his desk. I had no idea what was coming down the pike but I knew it could not be good.

In the quiet of his office he simply asked me why I had acted out? I told him my point of view and attempted to justify my behavior. The Professor just looked at me still smiling and told me what an exemplary student I was in college and how much many of the students looked up to me in general. He then he told me something I never forgot. He said, "If ninety-nine percent of the people love you, one percent would not simply because everybody else does." He said that I "was so busy worrying about what the one percent were thinking and doing" that I "had lost sight and appreciation for all the people who did care about me." I remember this because when the core issue came up again years later, I realized that I was still focused on the one percent and trying to fix them. Furthermore, the Professor informed me that the two ladies in the classroom were talking about clothes! I owed them a huge apology! And oh by the way, I had forgotten for many years that I had been a Lieutenant Fire Patrol in elementary school. My job was to be the last one out of the building in a fire drill and wave my arms in the air yelling, "All clear!"

❖ **Who are the hall monitors in your life?**

The above stories were formulated to show how a person who has an exaggerated sense of responsibility believes he or she has to help others "fix" everything. Some part of them always sees what is wrong with the *other* person(s) and what can be done to help them overcome their flaws. The *need to be needed* outweighs the understanding that it is time to let the other person take responsibility for his or her own journey in life. The conflict arises when one person believes the other person is not able to figure it out and "I can fix it or them!"

As long as the attention is focused on others we can avoid our own growth in order to ignore what motivates the programs (the inner stories). Sometimes it is more important to think we can do a better job of making someone else's movie than they can. And many times we attract people who do not want to take responsibility for their own movie and eager to have someone else direct it for them! As long as we are busy attempting to fix their movie, their life, then we do not have to take a closer look at what is happening in our own.

Hall monitoring is simply the ego of the personal mind attempting to deflect and shield the deeper core programs in our own lives. It becomes apparent when we take a look at ourselves that we will do anything to avoid who we really are and why we feel, think and act out with certain behaviors. But as long as the focus is outside the Self we avoid understanding our own life purpose.

❖ **What conflicting desires do you have?**

· *Do I vote or is it a waste of time?*
· *Do I help my friend or do I mind my own business?*
· *Should I marry him or should we just live together?*
· *Should I clean my house or should I stay in bed and watch TV?*
· *Do I work overtime or do I go to the gym?*

When we are in conflict with our desires, values or beliefs it will often mirror back to us as a need to blame others for their inner conflicts or the need to help someone else resolve his or her inner conflicts instead of resolving our own.

If we begin to take care of our own inner conflicts and only take responsibility for our own beliefs, desires and values and not others, the opportunity to establish healthy and positive boundaries will occur. We begin to know when it is time to say "yes" and when to say "no."

This ability is called discernment. Discernment is the quality to grasp the obscured. It is a level of discrimination that stresses an ability to distinguish between what is true or appropriate. It is the perception to know when a snake is a snake or a when a snake is in butterfly clothing.

Intuition is the key to this ability to see beyond the obvious into the obscured and interpret what is being presented to us in a manner that allows an opportunity to make the appropriate decision. Developing a keen sense is connected to a deeper understanding of discernment in trusting how we feel when confronted with growth.

How often has each one of us felt a concrete feeling about something and still decided on a course of action that we knew was inappropriate? Sometimes we say "yes" when we really want to say "no" only to later self-chastise for not listening to the messages within. If we continue along the path of ignoring how we feel, the inner dialogue will send a message to the personal mind saying, "I don't know if I can trust anything."

Developing a deeper connection with our inner feelings will save many hours of unwanted and inappropriate challenges. This connection is an exploration into the inner knower of who we are within.

Cooperation With Self

When we are in association with someone for mutual benefit we are in cooperation. The same applies when we are in association with our desires and our beliefs; we are in cooperation with Self.

When our beliefs are mirroring our desires we are in balance, or better yet, when we are in the flow, we are feeling good. However, the reverse is also true, and the mirror of our journey reflects it back to us every time.

We can always know first-hand whether we are in the flow of life by examining the now. Is my life today a *now* that I desire to be living? Do I feel good about today? "Well, sometimes 'yes' and often-times 'no'." When it is "no," then it is time to sit down and reflect on why the desires in my past are manifesting today? *What did I really believe about my future one year ago or last week? Obviously my desires were not in accord with what I really believe or I would be living that life today and feeling good about it.*

We cannot change the past; it only exists in our memory reel to guide us into our present and our future. What the past does well is give us the opportunity to understand why we are where we are today. This is the gift we are given each day.

If today is about feeling bored, stressful, anxious, unsafe, or a myriad of other lower vibrational feelings, it is only because we have attracted the feelings from how we felt before now.

෧ ෧ ෧

If you say, "I do not understand why I am not prosperous today", it is important to understand it is because all the moments leading up to now were filled with feeling unworthy. Feeling the lack of abundance in your life is directly related to not truly believing the Universe is here to give you everything you desire and that you *already* have it all. Your beliefs are not in alignment with how you are feeling. So instead of feeling anxious about what you presently do not have in your life, examine what it is you really believe about prosperity, abundance and self-worth. Begin by understanding you are not cooperating with your Self.

Take a deeper look at what your present life is mirroring back to you today. The fact is the lack of prosperity in your life is directly in line with your feelings of not being worthy to receive. See the lack of prosperity as a gift, to show you what part of your script in your movie needs rewriting. It is called the gift of *constructive criticism*.

Lacking anything is connected to lack of self-worth. "I am not prosperous because I am not worthy enough to receive prosperity." The universe you live in is not safe or peaceful and lacks the ability to give you what you really desire.

Not taking this examination personally is important. It can be a time to begin allowing yourself to receive, since you have not been doing it before. You can change the past; changing how you feel about it by writing a different script today. The opportunity is to know this and simply change the way you feel about yourself. *How do I do that?*

The first thing to do is to acknowledge your feelings of unworthiness! The second thing to do is to figure out why.

The why will be connected to your beliefs and most of the time the why is hiding in your *God box*. The God box is where you keep your concepts of what your belief in God is, and you carry the God box around in a very secret or private place in your thoughts. If you take a closer look inside the God box you can discover the *Who am I?* you perceive God to be.

ภ ภ ภ

Most of the time our perception of God is made from inherited family beliefs or is recreated out of rejecting those very same beliefs. Either way, we hold a collection of thoughts about who God is and why we are choosing to believe in him/her/them the way we do. As we know, there are many different *feelings* in the world about who or what God is, as there are as many gods. There are also as many *conflicts* about God as there are beliefs about God. And we already established that conflicts about everything are created out of individual *inner* conflicts.

· *Is God a loving God or a judgmental God?*
· *Does God love me unconditionally/conditionally, transparently?*
· *Am I co-creating with God or only a creation?*

50

- *Is God male/female or a Higher Consciousness expressing itself in me?*
- *Is God abundance or only giving me what I am allowing myself to receive?*
- *Am I co-creating through the Divine Will or only asking for redemption?*
- *Am I infinite and immortal or only a mortal in time and space?*
- *Do I deserve or do I allow?*
- *Is God infinite wisdom or a father/mother figure?*
- *Is God fixed or open and willing to grow?*
- *Do I believe in God or is this all there is to my life?*
- *Do I fear God, or only fear myself?*

❖ **Take a closer look in your God box and make a list of what your God beliefs really are, not the ones you think other people might wish to hear.**

❖ **Write down all the attributes of your God—what God looks like, acts like, and what God would say to you about your life right this moment.**

❖ **How does your God make you feel about yourself? How do you feel about your God? Do you feel good, scared, alone, fearful, curious, loved, or controlled?**

What do I believe?

Now ask yourself if your God allows you to feel good?

If the answer is anything less than feeling good about yourself, then it is time to take a deeper look at why you are choosing to have this God in your God box?

Do you feel abundant, prosperous, taken care of in all ways, and do you trust in the Divine Order? Is the Higher Consciousness already present within? Are you a co-creator (a part of everything) in your life or a victim (reacting to a perceived outer world)?

If on any level or at any degree your God is not behind you one hundred percent, then it is time to fire God and awaken something that allows you to feel good about yourself.

You may think that this is rationalizing, but ask yourself *what alternative do I have?*

ဖ ဖ ဖ

One of the reasons we are not able to create the things we truly desire is we do not feel safe in our world. Whether it is our feeling of a lack of prosperity or a lack of love, it all stems from how we connect in our beliefs to an abundant universe. If we feel the universe is not abundant, able and willing to give us our heart's desire, then it is a universe that is impotent. What we are attracting is the lack of love and the lack of abundance in wisdom.

If we believe our Self unworthy, then our universe will mirror our unworthiness. If we feel unloved and unsafe in the universe, then we will mirror feelings of being unloved.

What is mirrored back to us in the universe? *Am I in service or am I in servitude?*

Maybe it is time to create an intention, which is mutually beneficial for everyone in the universe.

Is my God belief in cooperation for the mutual benefit of all?

It is time for a reconnection with the God-Self, the *universal life force* which is the highest divine aspect of Self and is absolute abundance everywhere. The Universal Source provides all that we wish for in the best and highest good—the Source which vibrates peace and transparent love, guiding us in all ways without judgment and conditional/unconditional love.

Do you have a God belief that is cooperating with your heart's desire or a God that is a hall monitor?
Am I a receiver?

The world is made up of receivers and unwilling receivers who are both givers and takers.

The givers believe it is better to give than to receive. The takers believe it is what they deserve. In everyone there is a bit of both, a giver and a taker. What we think about our own and others' responsibilities often determines how we perceive our experience of cooperation.

In the world of the giver it is about the responsibility of giving time, energy and resources to the outside world. It is about being perceived as generous, loving and supportive. It is about giving to others, as they would like to be given. Then why is it often that the giver only appears to attract the takers, or why is the giver giving more than he or she receives?

Being a giver can sometimes feel good, and this feeling is the *addiction* to giving. Oftentimes being a giver allows us to enable others so we can feel needed and wanted. Other times it is just the way we are, the Good Samaritan, wanting to help out and feel connected to the world we are living in. When we feel the best is when we know we are giving out of a sense of being lovable. It becomes empowered giving!

But what happens when our giving is out of balance? What happens when the world we think we are cooperating with just seems to take and take and take? When is giving enough? *Why is it feeling as if someone always wants something from me?*

When the giving becomes imbalanced long enough a wonderful question might be asked, usually out of frustration!

When is it going to be my turn?

When anything gets far enough out of balance, the *Law of Balance*, the place between all polarities, will work to bring the balance back to the center—in our total Self the center is trust, the center is Love.

"When is it going to be my turn?" is the *Law of Balance* at work.

The question is asked rhetorically: "When is it going to be your turn?" The answer is "when you realize you are not cooperating with your Self."

The giver spends a great deal of time imbalanced. The giver does not understand how much resistance they are attracting from the *need* to be a giver. The giver is out of balance because of spending too much time giving to everybody else and very little time giving to themselves. The giver is mirroring resistance from the *Law of Balance* and feeling frustration and anxiety instead of feeling good. And what the giver ends up giving to the universe is a feeling of being over-extended and under-appreciated. The giver is, in the end and without knowing it, giving the world *frustration*.

Recovering balance of giving to others and giving to our Self is discovering how we receive.

· *I am open to receive.*
· *I am in gratitude for all that I receive that honors my integrity.*
· *I am willing to get what I ask for.*

· *All that I receive, I do so with warmth and graciousness.*
· *I am willing to receive from all sources.*
· *As I give, I receive.*
· *I honor the universe in its abundance.*
· *I give generously to myself.*
· *I already have all that I require to be healthy, prospered and fulfilled.*

The art of receiving is the completion of the circle of energy! It is the give and take, the yin and yang of the art of balance. Allowing the circle of energy to be completed is to allow infinite freedom of flow.

Many people believe that receiving is being selfish. But being selfish is only when we are thinking of ourselves by taking advantage of others. If we are receiving at the advantage of others, then we are probably giving for the same reason! It is important to look at how we give to others and why. Is there an agenda in the giving?

Are we giving to others with the *intention* of getting something in return? Love? Money? Time? Attention? Sexual favors?

Giving only vibrates at the highest level when it is *given* freely, whether it is for us or for anything or anybody else. It is when we give something of value we receive something of value in return.

· *Everything I give to others is a gift to myself.*
· *Everything I give to myself is a gift to others.*
· *Everything we are giving of value is a gift to the universe.*
· *Everything the universe is giving of value is a gift to us.*

People unwilling to receive freely justify many reasons for it. Most of the time the reasons are from lack of self-worth and other times from a lack of self-love, and sometimes a combination of the two.

Lack is the opposite of appreciation.

When our self-worth (moral and personal values) is in vibrational balance with our self-love (regard for one's own happiness) we are cooperating with our Self.

A connection to our spiritual Self will trust in our intuition (inner positive affirmed feelings), releasing all feelings of sadness and lack of personal abundance, health or fulfillment.

The more I am open to receive, the more I am able to give.

Givers, in the highest vibration, are giving to others to empower them. Every gift we give to others is given to empower them more. We are honoring and placing value towards them. It allows us to feel good about what we have given and feel good in the Soul.

Then why am I not manifesting the same gifts for myself?

The art of self-love is a state of knowing—realizing we are confident and satisfied with WHO I AM. Knowing is an awareness of value, all desirable characteristics, and self-esteem, which morally aligns us with our desires.

In the art of giving we are in balance with our Self and with others, transcending cooperation, with the higher awareness of seeing each person as part of the Higher Self. This resolves all inner conflict that previously led to resentments about over-giving and under-receiving for our life purpose.

· *I am the Divine Light within.*
· *The Divine Light and I are one.*

The Intuition Connection

Intuition is the ability to connect to knowledge without evident rational thought or interference. In other words, the ability to connect on the most profound level of our intuition is made through listening to what our "gut" is telling us. It is about getting out of the interference of the ego and personal mind, the constant chatter of the "thousand monkeys," and being sensitive to what we feel within.

The "rational" personal mind is telling us only to listen to what we think and respond to what we see, hear, touch, taste and smell. The rational personal mind or *monkey mind* is responding to the stimuli it is receiving from the outer world. More importantly, the monkey mind is very comfortable with the repeated thoughts we are thinking and replaying/reviewing throughout the day. No wonder the monkey mind is referred to as a "broken record"! If new thoughts are introduced, the monkey mind will decide if the thoughts can fit appropriately into the beliefs (collection of thoughts) that are already in place.

The intuition will reveal vibrations in the body from outside the parameters of our personal mind's *infused thoughts* into the very being of *Who I am* which in turn will ask for a response from our conscious awareness. The personal mind will then take the responsibility of deciphering (interfering) with this process, in order to decide whether or not it is something to listen to or to become reactive towards. The personal mind (the mental plane) is simply doing its job in attempting to decipher all the monkey chatter bubbling up!

The problem is the personal mind is unable to truly decipher the biology of feelings without first putting them in the constructs of what it rationally knows. The mind observes the information and determines it to be of unknown sources and therefore not valid. The personal mind will then tell us the information is invalid.

What happens next all depends on how connected we are to listening to our intuition. The less connected we are to our deeper feelings the more likely we are—determined through either conscious choice or reactive victimization—not to pay attention to what we are deeply feeling. Normally we will decide that whatever our personal mind tells us is good advice especially if the thousand monkeys cavorting in our head distract us!

The more in touch we are with our feelings, the more likely we will disregard our mind's judgment on the validity of the feelings and trust what we are feeling is valid. *I know that I know, but I do not know why accepts and trusts what we feel is worthwhile.*

Most people are the middle range.

· *I should have listened to what I felt but my mind said, "Listen to me!"*
· *Something told me not to do that but I did it anyway!*
· *My friend said turn right yet I felt I should turn left!*
· *Damn! I should have listened to my hunches!*
· *I heard them say one thing but I knew the other was truer.*
· *If I had only followed my instinct, I would be happier!*
· *I don't trust my feelings because every time I do I get hurt!*
· *It feels right but it isn't logical!*
· *If I had listened to myself, I wouldn't be in this predicament!*

Spiritual development is the journey through enhancing the awareness of the more subtle experience of the quality of life. In order to delve into the deeper meanings—in other words which vibrations are injected into our being—we must first be open to feeling what we feel, without reservation and without determination in accepting the rational ego's and the personal mind's opinion. After all an opinion is just another word for *judgment*.

Allowing the feelings on a deeper level to flow effortlessly will significantly elevate our psychic awareness into higher dimensional vibration so we can tap into the region of creative expression. Without interference from the personal mind we touch the more spiritual essence in our personal perception of our agreements with the Universal Mind or Higher Consciousness of the Self.

Intuition is not about bypassing the mind but affirming to our Self there is another gateway to inner knowing beyond what our outer senses express.

The opportunity to tap into this deeper pool of meaning can be easily realized the moment we set our intention toward developing what we cannot understand and knowing we can know what we feel is just as valid as what we think. Affirming without justifying allows the Universal Mind to *infuse* the personal mind, which in turn will affirm (created affirmations) to the subconscious (the magnetic attractor). We can then begin to get out of our way and align our discernment with conscious positive affirming thoughts.

- *I know what I feel and I trust it.*
- *I am one with my inner feelings.*
- *I am tapping into the Source of my own creativity.*
- *I have a higher purpose and I will listen to the song in my Soul.*
- *My spirit, mind and body are in cooperation.*
- *I am co-creating with my higher purpose.*
- *I am open and willing to receive all that I am.*
- *What I feel is in alignment with what I think.*

Setting aside time for meditation and spiritual reading are the cooperation required for developing awareness of the intuition.

Meditation can be as easy as sitting quietly, with eyes closed, aware of the ebb and flow of breathing. It can be as effortless as watching a candle flicker and dance.

Meditation can be the art of reflection and being still. It can be the act of *being still* and quieting the mind while allowing the inner life to explore a calmer world, a world filled with infinite possibilities that are safe and loving.

In the journey of discovering meditation it is valuable to spend twenty to thirty minutes a day in the art of reflection. At first it appears easier to be in the busy world of thinking and doing, the world of habits and blunt energies, but this is not true. When we connect our Self into the deeper love, the outer world becomes more than what the five senses can know. The outer world becomes the dance and the inner world becomes the song.

Through meditation and quieting the mind, we begin to take greater control of what we understand about who we are. The art of meditation allows us to cooperate and balance with the inner and outer worlds to begin realizing they are complete.

It may take time and patience to see the deeper world we travel in, but it is worth the time and the intention we place in discovering the total Self.

Some will say they have trouble meditating, that it is too hard to sit still. They have tried to meditate but nothing happens and they feel as though they are wasting time! It is interesting that most of the time these same people only relate to how disconnected they are from what they feel, because all their feelings are bottled up and ready to explode! What they are really saying is *I don't know how to feel about anything!*

The possibility of so many feelings swelling up inside and exploding is only reserved for people who are frustrated and continue the conflict between the inner and outer worlds.

More the reason to sit down and shut up! Because the resistance is, *I am not allowing myself to receive.*

ʂ ʂ ʂ

It is beneficial to allow yourself time to reflect upon your inner world, by minimally making meditation a once-a-day reflection. Schedule twenty minutes a day. You can divide the time if necessary between morning and night. I find the morning to be the best time because it allows me to set my positive affirmed intentions for the day.

Start the day with the opportunity to feel great about your day. Spend a few minutes in bed awake. Let your mind think about all the things in your life you hold in gratitude and appreciation. Spend a few minutes thinking about all the gifts you have been given, all the gifts you *already* have, and continue to receive. Then sit up in bed and spend time in quietness. Allow your thoughts to flow effortlessly. If you begin to hold an idea too long, blow it away and allow the thoughts to bubble up rhythmically. Whenever you become anxious or embedded in one group of thoughts, shift your awareness to your breathing. Listen, feel and participate in the flow of breath moving in and out of your body. It is not important to focus on any one thought or group of thoughts. Your intention is to spend quality time with your Self and to simply receive.

Another technique is to sit quietly and become aware of the breath moving in and out of the lungs. After a couple of minutes turn your attention to the "third eye" and observe the colors that may come and go. If the chatter starts up in your personal mind say to yourself, "It is only the chatter of a thousand monkeys," and then allow your awareness to once again turn to your third eye watching and observing the colors swirl in your mind's eye. If there is anything bothering you, a problem that disturbs your peace of mind, simply say to your Self, "I am safe." Say it several times until you begin to feel peaceful. Take a few minutes to open your eyes allowing them to adjust to the outer senses before getting up and moving around.

You can also end the session with, "Thank you for this healing." This exercise, along with Reiki will become a valuable part of your daily routine.

ᔆ ᔆ ᔆ

· *I am flowing effortlessly and easily in my life.*
· *I am the Divine Light within me.*
· *I am open and willing to grow.*
· *I am open and willing to receive.*
· *I am grateful for all the gifts I receive for my highest good.*
· *I am safe.*
· *I am willing to heal my life every day.*
· *I am in the flow of life.*
· *My inner and outer worlds are in cooperation.*
· *I love who I am.*
· *I appreciate and value myself.*

❖ **I will meditate every day.**

Meditation connects us to the vibrations that allow enhancement of wisdom through growth in conscious awareness. Adding spiritual reading as an accessory tool will enhance the Soul by validating our deepest inner feelings.

ᔆ ᔆ ᔆ

The quantity of spiritual material available to everyone is abundant. How do you sort through all the data, especially if you do not consider yourself much of a reader?

Easy! First, connect with the center point on your journey. Then, examine what the issues are that you wish to clarify and "clear" to improve the quality of your personal movie called *My Life*. Next, march yourself into the nearest spiritual bookstore and talk to the owner. Tell that person exactly what is going on in your life at this moment and how you feel about it. The owner will listen, and then smile, while strolling you over to whatever section of the bookstore you require. After spending a little time thumbing through the material your intuition will tell you which book to read. If you are still not sure whether to listen to what you are feeling, you can do a test on yourself to see if your body agrees.

ᔕ ᔕ ᔕ

It is called "muscle testing". When our heart is not sure what to feel and our mind is always busy telling us what to feel there is another opportunity to listen within.

It is with the human body! Whatever is going on in the mind or heart is always received and validated in the body. The body never lies to us! We may not have the wisdom to interpret what the body is attempting to tell us, but the physical body gets every message we send ourselves and translates it into *who* we are in the flesh.

ᔕ ᔕ ᔕ

Take a moment in the bookstore and stand in the aisle with your legs shoulder width apart. Close your eyes and whisper "yes." Immediately afterwards, lean forward. Go back to center and whisper "no." Then lean backwards. Your body now understands that when you want it to say "yes" your body will sway forward and when you want it to say "no" you will sway backwards. This process may take a little time as you get the body in alignment with your feelings and thoughts. The more you allow yourself to trust what you are doing, the faster the results—you will be surprised how fast the answers will be received. Now once again close your eyes and whisper your name and feel which way your body sways. If you sway forward you are ready to muscle test your book of choice. Ask yourself, "Is this book for my best and highest good?" Feel which direction your body sways. If it is "yes," then ask, "Should I read it now?" If you sway forward again, then you have the book that will help guide you through your present desire to expand your awareness of whatever it is you need to understand so the vibration you are in may be elevated.

There are all types of bookstores. Some stores have a New Age section; some stores only carry specific sections. It is important to connect with a bookstore that feels good to you when you enter. If for any reason the store feels differently leave and find the one that allows you to feel safe and to feel good.

Just remember, you desire to cooperate and find balance in your life. The life you are living today is open and willing to grow. The life you are living today is asking you to allow yourself the opportunity to change. By connecting with meditation and spiritual reading every day, you will be provided with the tools and feelings to create the future feelings you desire.

I listen to the wisdom of my heart.

Cooperating With My Guides

For thousands of years, hundreds of texts, scriptures, poems and pictures reference to people talking to "Beings" that are "not of this world." There have been soothsayers, shamans, medicine people and religious figures whom all have had visions, prophesies spoken in dreams, and sometimes even figures who have appeared to tell stories.

The values of all such experiences and teachings have been interpreted by societies for generations. Yet, so often the ones who speak, see, feel or experience messages are either ridiculed or praised depending on the agenda of the observers.

The general public has always held that only a few, crazy or otherwise, have such an ability to talk to the gods or demons depending on the god beliefs they personally hold. It is also held that none of these experiences were ever to be completely understood by the general public but only by a select few.

Religions by and large have written bylaws either banning or denying the ability of being able to communicate with anything outside what the five senses can interpret. Witches, soothsayers, religious figures and average villagers have been burned, beheaded, drowned, and ridiculed in observation by their communities. Whether it was fear or the fear of different beliefs, the collective consciousness of the planet has supported this behavior in the past and many still are crusading around today. Obviously, there have been many who have supported and developed such seers in societies but the general movement has been the opposite. It is unfortunate that in most of the western religions today, the members are instructed not to listen or interact with any spiritual teachings outside of their religious doctrine and go as far as to state they are forbidden. I personally find it fascinating that such extreme beliefs are enforced by the very religious leaders who use such words as "prophesy," "miracle" and "vision" to teach mystical allegory—foundations that are based on visions of prophets and forecasting by teachers.

Because such collective thinking is re-enforced in societal teaching and dogma as "woo-woo," the pursuit to connect with our own individual inner "voice" communications is stifled in the education of the masses. Political and religious leaders have insisted the whole business is either hocus-pocus or evil! I also find it interesting that mostly men fuel both types of thought manipulation.

When there is any talk of intuition by and large it has been women who follow the more feminine energies connected with this very feeling oriented guidance. This is not to suggest that men are not intuitive, but normally it is an energy that has been associated with the feminine energies. Men who are in touch with their feminine energies know very well how important it is to connect with the feeling guided intuition.

I bring all this up because of how important it may be for all of us to understand the nature of intuition. The not so subtle energies associated with each and every one of us can make the difference in developing the necessary steps to creating everything from our best and highest good or those things which serve only to manifest hardship and lessons based on archaic ideas about mystical experiences.

Connecting with the deeper feelings which express whether we feel good about something, or uneasy and unhappy about something, will determine *every time* how the co-creative process with Self and with others will flow. Connecting with the deeper feelings is joy and happiness infused with whatever it is we desire. Intuition is the next important step after conscious-aware-positive-affirmed-deliberate-intentions to co-create from the highest possible vibration to creation!

Knowing how we feel about anything will determine how graciously and effortlessly we will allow it to manifest.

Intuition is communicating with the I Am God-Mind, Higher Self, Higher Consciousness, Natural Universe or any other term suited to understanding All THAT IS beyond the personal mind and the ego (edging God out!). The higher self is what is in our best and highest good and our joy. The more we allow our Self to listen to our God song, the clearer life will appear.

We can always ask our Self how we feel about anything we are about to create. Many people will skip this step or continue forging ahead even though they are not feeling good about it. Whether it be to please someone else or because their *human will* believes it needs it, the outcome will always be the teaching and understanding of the lessons to bring the human will into balance with the ALL THAT IS. It is the choice to act anyway we want. It is the universe's nature to balance everything in perfection for the best and highest good of the universe, which may not be what we think we want at the time. The universe is acting in the highest good for all even when the all is acting only for itself!

When we are communicating with our higher self through the channel of our feelings, we are creating our highest vibration. When we are in doubt of what we are feeling we can always talk to our guides.

Guides? Who are they? I like to think of them as the production assistances (P.A.'s) on our movie sets. They are the least paid and most overworked part of our movie. They take care of all the small details that overwhelm the cast and crew—without them there would be no picture. Just like in the motion picture industry, production assistances should be treated with respect, and always treated with politeness. Because just like the movies, they can quit and then where will the movie be? What kind of chaos will ensue?

Guides come in all shapes and sizes. They can be familiar soul family energies or larger than life universal life forces appearing like energy fields with color arrays or angels. Guides are familiar dreams that beckon and speak to us in familiar voices we know, and even in the form of the old time sci-fi aliens we keep hoping will return. Well just like the aliens, what makes us believe any of these energies have ever left?

We are channeling all the time, whether we believe it or not. We are communicating with "others" whether we think we are or not. And we are given guidance, whether we receive it or not.

Who am I talking to in my head?

As I said before, I prefer to think of them as production assistances or P.A.'s. I know without them the movie of my life would be very difficult to create. And I have learned that cooperating with them is as important as cooperating with my cast and crew. Without being patronizing or attached, it is important to treat everyone who is helping us make our movies with the highest respect. They don't have to be here working or guest starring in our movies; they have their own My Life In The Universe movie to make. Whether they are co-workers, children, parents, lovers, friends or acquaintances, they can quit, walk away and let us figure it out all for ourselves. It is self-centered for anyone to believe they are doing it all themselves. Most of the time, those are the very people who are letting someone else direct their life. It seems easier to them. If anything goes wrong they can blame someone else!

We are co-creating with our Self, our Higher Self and every one else! If we are creating, we are delegating, learning, communicating and progressing only because everyone else is doing the same thing and with the same collaborators. No one does it alone and no one gets left behind. We are one and same.

Intuition is *knowing* you are connected to every great talent in the universe. The best doctors, lawyers, spiritual advisors, chefs, artists, scientists, manifesters, generators, projectors and caregivers are in our universe. And they are all here to help us understand that *we will never be alone*. If we are disconnected to our intuition we *think*, "I am alone on an unsafe world." Being connected to our *deepest* feelings we know that we *know* whether we believe it or not.

Intuition is connected on the emotional/spiritual *plane* (a field of energy) with our heart center and it is balanced by wisdom through abundance. The heart center is where we open to trust. If all three are open and in balance, the emotional/spiritual center of our being is in harmony with our Higher Self, Higher Consciousness—natural universe and joyful being.

Sacred Geometry In Numbers

In this book we will take a look at how numbers are part of our spiritual toolbox to conscious, positive affirmed living. Vibrationally, numbers can help us understand what aspects we are working with to attract (magnetize) exactly what it is we require to take in all the steps to fulfilling our life purpose or our smallest desire to completion. Numerology is one such opportunity to do just that and it is why I have placed this tool in our spiritual toolbox.

I am not spending a great deal of time covering all there is to know about numerology. There are many great books and teachers who are adept in the use of numbers and I have listed recommended books in the appendix for your consideration. I love numerology and have used it in my practice for years. Please take the time to learn more about what numerology can do for you. I cannot say why it works but only know that I have applied many techniques taught by many teachers over the years and have found the results to be the same. For our purposes I will cover some of the aspects of numerology that may help in guiding us to understanding why we skip, resist or avoid certain steps on our journey.

Briefly, numerology has been around for thousands of years in some form or another. The Science of Numbers we will be examining comes from the great school of Pythagoras, born in 608 B.C.

Pythagoras founded his university at Crotona, a small Greek colony in southern Italy. His motto was "Know thyself, then thou shalt know the universe and God." He believed and taught to anyone who wanted to know more about self, understanding life purpose and how to work in harmony through the Science of Numbers. He knew that the balance of the universe depended upon physical, mental and spiritual components as reflected in human life.

Numerology can help us better know our Self and to know and understand the people around us in our life. Each of us strives for emotional, financial, healthy and fulfilled lives in a loving and joyful way.

Chapters One through Nine of this book are dedicated to sacred numbers and how each vibration reflected in the numbers can help us to understand who we are and how valuable our creative consciousness is as it unfolds.

We are expanding our consciousness on the leading edge of our universe at the same rate we are expanding our awareness.

We are on the leading edge of our personal expression as co-creators.

To understand numerology and the meaning of the numbers

as revealed by Pythagoras 2,500 years ago, it is important to have a *basic* idea of what each number means. (The meanings of each number can be studied in more depth with more understanding. This is just the icing on the cake. I am using the numbers and the chart as a tool to examine why some lessons keep repeating in our lives.)

ZERO is not considered a number but a symbol. It represents the Divine expression of Who I Am. It also represents the support given by the universe in our "work." I consider this symbol to represent the abundant support available from Guides. Guides are the Highest Consciousness of the Universe expressed as spiritual teachers, mentors, avatars, and angels. Guidance also is expressed in the Natural Laws to align us in positive awareness while navigating from lower to higher consciousness. The Laws like the Guides are present not to punish but to teach. The mistakes we create are simply learning tools showing us that we are making changes (shifts) in our consciousness. The idea that no one is required to do more than they can handle is reflected in this symbol. Zero also represents the Hero in Archetypes. It is the journeyman beginning the journey unabashed, uninhibited and confident. It is remarkable to see the present shift in Universal guidance with the birth of all the children now embarking in the 21st century. Note how many zeros are present in the birth charts of children now.

ONE is the first number in the gateway to the physical plane. It is the Divine expression in the universe, a microcosm of All That Is. One is the communicator of the Divine and is manifest in the physical plane. It is the first expression of the manifest individualized with the infinite potential of expressing

itself into the many. This is where the personality begins and the ego develops the programs that imprint our personal identity. All things become possible in the seed of intention with the One and the opposite of the one can occur in expressing the lack of all things. Depending on the amount of Ones in your birth chart will determine how much you have a need to be needed and reflected by others.

TWO is the first number in the gateway to the spiritual plane, or emotional level of the Self. It is the collaborator who reflects itself in partnership. It also represents balance and cooperation with the inner and outer world. In the duality of itself it speaks to itself in the form of intuition. Two is the collaborator who sees its reflection in the mirror and knows it is One and the same. The Two reflects itself and knows the reflection is only a mirror of Who I Am. If the mirror is perceived as opposition in the mind's eye the distraction by the image is distorted and balance is not attained. The Two does not see the gift of the message (image) instead reacts to it believing the reflection from life is not created first within. The number of Twos determines the depth of the field of intuition and the opportunity to listen to the small voice within. Meditation is a great tool for listening.

THREE is the first number in the gateway to the conscious self, or mental plane. It is the primary vibration of verbal expression and communication connected to the creative consciousness of mind. All thoughts bubble up into expression from the creative pool of Source. Thoughts as ideas become *form* though action. In Zero we have the un-manifest all knowing *energy* expressed (1.) In the One as the Self. (2.) Propelled into cooperation and balance as the Two being the intuitive *intelligence*. (3.) Guiding *thought* through the portal of the mind in the Three. The Three is symbolically represented as a triangle— the trinity of soul-mind-body—and also represented as fire—the creatively fueled expression which first must be ignited. It is also represented as the creative God-Mind that is always present yet only seen when a spark invokes it. The Three also is where clarity or Self-doubt is developed. The ability to discern (to see and understand the difference) in what is the best opportunity for growth by understanding what may or may not work for us. The orators, singers, painters, poets, writers and scientists, as well as the *muses* (guiding genius) dwell here to explore the possibilities of all events that may be put into action. The left lobe of the brain will create harmony through creativity balanced with the right side of the brains involvement with clarity and reason. As we can see—if the seed of intention in the One is planted and then nurtured in the Two through correctly interpreting (listening) to what intuition is suggesting—clarity and creative expression can flow freely in the Three vibration. We can begin to understand the importance of not missing these vital steps before manifesting any further on.

FOUR is the second physical plane number after the One and represents the center of the plane rooted in developing a strong foundation. The Four is solid and practical and the first building block in developing commitment from a plan in its physical instrument. The rock on which we stand in our human Self inspired by the divine. Symbolically it is the square and represents Earth and elemental. The Four is *Gaia* (Earth energy) and intensifies the emotional and practical fields through grounding. It empowers the intentions and plans of the One, Two and Three in being assured of success through commitment to form. When the Four energy is not present we sway towards being impractical, unsure and sometimes, we sign a contract without reading the small print only to be made more aware from the mistakes that follow. When the Four is multiplied it becomes more rigid and fixed, rooting Self in an unwillingness to change becoming stuck. The Four is about affirming growth through grounding and developing stability with a strong foundation but can also create an unwillingness to expand through movement especially when there are many Fours present in a birth chart. The need for wanting to be extremely practical can become mulish, or unreasonably inflexible.

FIVE is the second emotional plane number and at the center of the soul and vibrates through trust. It connects all the vibrations as the resonation of constants in change. It represents the all changing and ever present. In the *Tao*, the book of changes, the Five is the symbol of the pentagram and the transformation of life. The pentagram as illustrated by Leonardo da Vinci's drawing of a human with arms and feet spread in the shape of a star. We are star children imprinted with the same material as the universe. The Five reminds us to trust in knowing that Truth is liquid and ever changing. The parable of the Buddha speaks of the great *aha* realized in sitting under the Tree of Life and observing the river runs through it. The river represents all that is present yet moving in the way water flows. The only thing constant is change. Five also is the vibration of Love evolving into Higher Love through trusting the validity of life. It is also freedom explored through discipline, such as developing a healthy center by being charitable to others less fortunate, developing a psychic-physical bond through the practice of meditation, yoga, dancing or any other physical healing program which offers the soul-mind-body connection. When there are many Fives present in a birth chart a person can be overly sensitive feeling "hurt" like a stabbing in the heart. Trusting others more than we trust ourselves may create a hardship and suffering on the heart, which tells the personal mind to put the heart in a box to protect it. When the Five is missing in the birth chart it creates empathic ability attracting all feelings to the heart. If the empathic (a person who not only feels what they are feeling but what everyone else is feeling too) is without trust they feel emotionally imbalanced and unstable caused from the inability to discern the emotions of others from their own feelings).

SIX is the center of the mental plane and is all things in *application* of the Mind to hold the vision of Self Love. It also represents all relationships of Love in all aspects. It is the balancing of the left and right lobes of the brain, connecting the creative flow of thought through application to purpose. Applying anything is how we grasp ideas and continue building what the Five (trust) and Four (commitment) have made firm in the Six (faith —walking in the direction of our prayer) knowing we are safe and secure on our unseen journey to purpose. Without holding the vision through focused intention we may not create what purpose holds for us. A muddled future is a future unimagined. When we are able to apply symbolically or physically through thought what it is we want to create as if it has already been created, then we are able to continue the work since we already know the outcome. A loving relationship with others is only enhanced through a loving relationship to the Self. The Self is the very first relationship we are having with God co-creating within. When we love our Self, we love God. When we love life, life will love us back. However, the Six is also the worrywart and can reduce self-love to feelings of victimization. Sometimes reflected in feeling a lack of appreciation from others which may resound as "poor me." It is important to understand that this can be seen as an opportunity rather than an obstacle to self-love.

SEVEN is the mystical number. Seven chakras, days, and the I AM in the manifest word of God. Pythagoras considered seven to be the most sacred number. It is the philosopher and the vibration of understanding usually found through self-sacrifice (giving of oneself or one's interest for others). It is any understanding through direct experience rather than through the experiences of others. This type of learning through one's own life work can lead to becoming a great teacher because direct experience is often times the best education. Seven represents being open and willing to learn from one's own journey as well as others through shared understanding of experiences. Having one or more sevens in a birth chart emphasizes self-sacrifice and patience explored through personal works and experiences rather than understanding gained from others and may result in a process of repeating the work several times before understanding the lesson. If you have one or more Sevens in your birth chart, examine where you experience self-sacrifice in love, prosperity or health. Seven is also the know-it-all number and has no problem letting you know it! Often the largest obstacle for the Seven is sharing with others their own personal feelings about themselves. This can be due to feelings of guilt, shame or blame directed inwardly.

EIGHT is the wisdom number on the emotional plane and

opposite side of intuition. Often misrepresented as the prosperity number connected to financial wealth, in actuality it has more in common with abundance inherent in wisdom. Eight vibrates from the wisdom of knowing that whatever we know is from the abundant reservoir of infinite universal mind rather than from the material "land of more." Knowledge springs forth from the Sevens understanding—through self-sacrifice—the "work." This in turn initiates the Eight in *knowing* that all creation and infinite possibility reside in the universal mind of God. When the Eight energy is connected to abundance from a place of "entitlement" or "deserving," it will become overly ambitious and manifest as a "taker." Greed is an addiction to living in the "Land of More" and stems from a lack of self worth and self-esteem and has the need to prove there is value in the some *thing* rather than in the Self. We see this now with the use of the Law of Attraction being used to have "more" rather than the wisdom of its spiritual applications. Eight's vibration is the opportunity to find value in all creation as the living reflection of God and equal in and unto its Self. True knowledge is in knowing that when we give something of value to others we receive value in return.

NINE encompasses all other numbers and resides on the mental plane as the conscious Self through *purpose*. It is the vibration leading to the adept who is becoming complete. The Nine represents both the positive relationship of responsibility and idealism or may vibrate negatively to the dogmatic and extreme. At its highest vibration it is the spiritual leader guiding others who have not yet developed all aspects of every vibration. Encompassing all the numbers the Nine relates to each aspect through the full experience of the human condition offering the ability to be a lighthouse for all. The Nine energy promotes the ability to be a consummate light worker and manifester. Showing diligence and perseverance in causation. If the Nine is working from several same numbers it can become very dogmatic and fanatical expressing determination about truth with righteous indignation. The Nine has the opportunity to enjoy the journey of all the other numbers having already experienced the revelations and teachings of each vibration. As a spiritual teacher this vibration applies wisdom and application to the tools necessary to support life. In the negative the Nine can be the over achiever determined to build rather than nurture.

This is a very short and general outline of the Science of Numbers. It is here to give you a simple understanding of how vibrations from thought may create the attractions necessary for growth in consciousness. With the numbers in our birth chart we can begin to understand what tools we already are giving from the Self and expressing in our life. They represent the skills on our journey we can apply to co-create with life. The numbers missing in our birth chart are simply the vibrations we are attracting from animate and inanimate life to instruct us in the spiritual laws of the universe.

ꝯ ꝯ ꝯ

Apply the above number information to the following calculations to see what numbers you have present in you birth date and which ones are absent.

First write out your birth date in a line.

4-16-1972

Next add all the numbers across.

4 + 1 +6 +1 +9 +7 +2

Total up the numbers making sure you have separated them out.
30 = 3 + 0 = 3

This is your Birth Chart number that reflects the vibration you entered into the world. THREE is your number supported by the symbol ZERO.

Next make a blank tic-tac-toe chart.

Use the above filled chart as an example of where to place your existing numbers on your chart, and leave the spaces blank for missing numbers.

Some numbers will be duplicated in spaces so be sure to place them side-by-side as shown in the example above where I have placed two Ones.

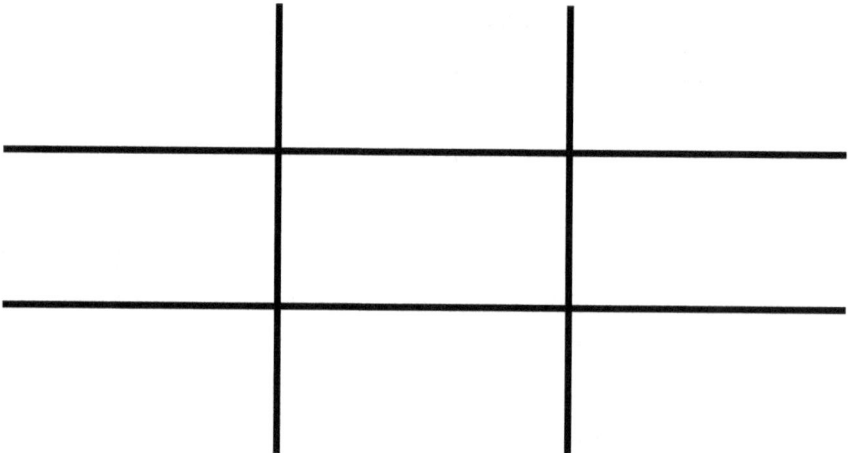

2:1

	6	9
2		
1	4	7

2:2

33	6	9
2	5	8
1	4	7

2:3

After you have plugged in the numbers of your birth chart take a look at the chart and figure out what numbers you have and which are missing. Utilizing this chart will help in understanding what you are emitting (giving) with the numbers present in your birth date and what the missing numbers represent in the vibrations you are attracting (receiving).

How many numbers do you have on the different planes? The bottom plane is your physical plane. The middle is your emotional plane and the top is your mental plane.

The <u>absent</u> <u>numbers</u> represent the steps you are required to pay attention to on your journey. It is easy to avoid these steps and usually in doing so you miss important work. The absent numbers are what you are magnetizing to yourself. The numbers that are part of your birth date represent what you are giving or emitting out into the world.

For example, if you are missing the FIVE, it becomes a vibration you are attracting in your life. FIVE represent Love, and Trust. As you can see, it is connected to all the other numbers, so without the FIVE, there may be trust issues connected to how you work with the other number vibrations. The empty FIVE means it is your journey to learn to trust yourself and connect with and center in your heart. Without trust, it is difficult to know if anything you are doing is of true value. If you do not trust yourself it may be harder to trust others, or if in conflict with the Self it can manifest as depending on

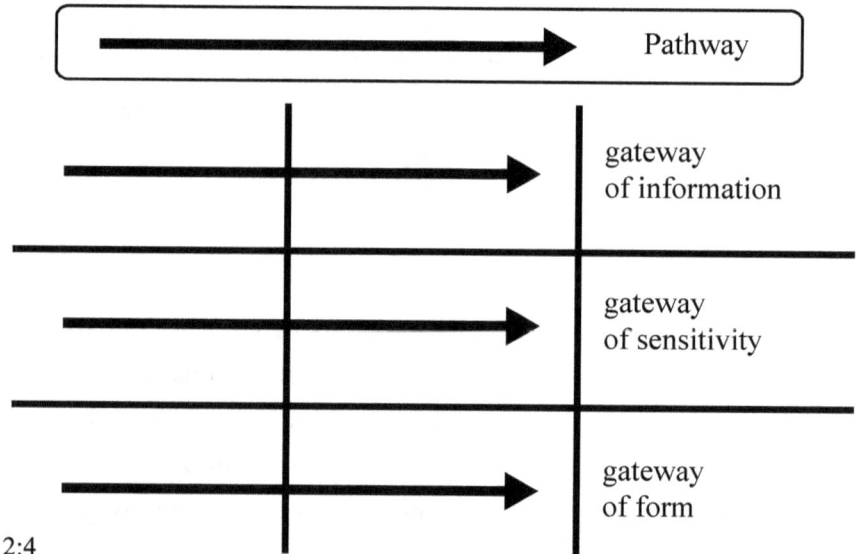

Pathway

gateway
of information

gateway
of sensitivity

gateway
of form

2:4

Positive

energy creativity	vision self-love	purpose manifestation
intuition cooperation	freedom trust	wisdom abundance
seeds of deliberate intentions	commitment stability	"the work" understanding

Where to apply discernment.

Negative

blocks self-doubt	worry victim	martyr procrastination
imbalance insensitive	insecurity deception	lack alienation
seeds of unaware intentions	impatiences stubbornness	shame self-sabotage

2:6

others trust to the detriment of personal growth.

Each vibration will be covered in further depth throughout the book. As you gain a deeper understanding of each chapter and the meaning of each number you will begin to see how each number relates to your vibrational journey of co-creating through giving and receiving.

Remember, the absence of any number does not necessarily mean you do not have the vibrational energy field. It simply means you are required to pay special attention to the process and not skip those steps within the process from intention to manifestation.

Another example is that I am missing the four in my chart. I spent years rebelling against being practical and committing to anything. Interestingly enough my mother had the four in her chart and was always telling me that I needed to be more practical and more responsible for my financial well being. Of course I did not listen to her because I thought I could get along without such notions! I attracted her to my life to teach and inspire me to understand the value of the Four vibration and to learn from this step. Of course I resisted this step because of believing I could get along without this knowledge. It took years for me to realize she was absolutely on point. But for some reason I thought I could skip this step in my journey and develop without it! Well I did grow, but the growth came from pain and hardship instead of acceptance and allowance previously offered over and over again. My resistance of being impractical and non-committal taught me to take the time to learn the true value of building a strong foundation!

We get the value of life either way assuring that the choice is how we determine the way we want to get it! There is no wrong or right way spiritually. The universe is not here to judge, but to grow and expand in the oneness of God or Higher Consciousness through awareness. A mistake can be viewed as negative if awareness is limited or it can be experienced as the opportunity to create change in our growth in consciousness.

· *I am open and willing to receive.*
· *Everything is for my best and highest good.*
· *I allow myself to go through my process.*
· *I AM co-creating my movie through the universal mind of God.*
· *I ask and receive for my best and highest good.*

· *I share and evolve from mutual understanding.*
· *I listen to the small quiet voice within.*

Discovery

1. Hall monitors need to make sure everyone else is doing "right"! Hall monitors believe they are here to fix everyone else's mistakes or to make sure others do not do it "wrong" in the first place. Who are the hall monitors in your life?

2. When you are in conflict with your desires, values or beliefs it will often mirror back to you as a need to blame others for their own inner conflicts. It will also mirror the need to help someone else resolve his or her inner conflicts instead of resolving your own. What conflicting desires do you have?

3. I will meditate everyday! Take a moment everyday to be still. Quiet yourself and begin to reflect on your inner journey through the universal mind and heart center. A candle, a silent prayer, breathing energy in and energy out, or simply sit in a chair and be still. Let the thoughts come in and the thoughts go out. Do not think you need to stop thinking but instead simply be still and become empowered though knowing that whatever you require is already known by the highest consciousness.

4. Take a moment to calculate the birth dates of family and friends to reflect on the abundance you are receiving everyday and also what you are giving to others in return. It is also fun to take the final number of each person in your immediate world to see what all the numbers tally together.

This is the vibration and energy collectively being created. For example: Your birth date is 4-12-1960 = 4+1+2+1+9+6+0=23. 2+3=5. Your final number is a five (5). Now add up the birth dates of all those in your immediate life and add the final number together of everybody to see what you are creating together.

Everyday Affirmations

I am open to receive.

I am in gratitude for all that I receive that honors my integrity.

I am willing to get what I ask for.

All that I receive I do so with warmth and graciousness.

I am willing to receive from all sources.

As I give, I receive.

I honor the Universe in its abundance.

I give generously to myself.

Everything I give to others is a gift to myself.

The more I am open to receive, the more I am able to give.

I am my Divine Light within.

Go confidently in the direction of your dreams.
Live the life you have imagined.
- Henry David Thoreau

Chapter 3: Creativity

Expression

Expression is fueled by Energy, directed by Intelligence and manifested in Thought.

Expression creates *something* that is then manifested, embodied or symbolized as *something else*. The "something else" is our desire actualized. From the deepest pool of our being, thoughts are created and then expressed. Which thoughts become realities depends on where we focus our intentions.

We are creating every moment of every day, and what we create is always our own responsibility. The thoughts we have are ours, *and only ours*—no one else's. Even if everyone else is having similar thoughts, the thoughts only become our own thoughts when we attach to them. Attaching to any of these thoughts is our individual choice.

When we make the choice to attach to any of the millions of thoughts bubbling up from Source every second, we are expressing our Self-expression and the assertion of our own individual traits, our personality.

Expression realized, in Self-expression, is our ability to co-create with our Source, the Higher Self.

What is interesting, however, is how many people do not believe that they are creative. Interestingly enough, every choice they are making is being creative whatever it may be they wish to create or not create. People are creating their own manifested destiny every day, without conscious understanding of it!

The Art of Expression flows at the highest vibration when there is no interference from the filter of self-doubt. The denser the filter of uncertain belief or any restrictive opinions interfering, the more untrusting the judgment becomes in what is being expressed.

Any uncertainty is rooted in fear.

Fear is the alarm-emotion alerting an anticipation of danger or dread. Fear is a very potent emotion! Fear is the emotional anticipation filtering the ability to express clearly. Fear is the ultimate Dream Stealer! Therefore, the amount of fear we emotionally express with our desires, the stronger the blocks placed in front of our creativity, the more over-sensitivity and self-doubt will distort our expression.

We express ourselves in various ways. Expression is manifested in creative consciousness. Painting and dancing are types of non-verbal expressions. Writing and singing are verbal. Expression is also manifested in the sciences. Numbers and analysis express thoughts from abstract ideas. Yet, the most commonly used expressions are created from words.

The Art of Communication is manifested in the human ability to express thoughts as words.

Expression, most commonly, is _fueled_ by Energy, _directed_ by Intelligence and _manifested_ as Thought in action through words and deeds.

The Art of Expression is often something manifested, embodied or symbolized as thoughts *compounded* by emotional-expression, the "something else," before words are expressed.

Emotional expressions are the feelings of fear (hate or anger), love, joy and sadness, attached to words. Every word created with an attached emotional expression is manifested as a lower or higher vibration in the Universe.

How important do you believe your responsibility is in manifesting emotional expressions as words?

Thoughts as words are deeds and a deed is something that is done.

Words are how we express our Self the most often. Words are a mirror of who we are. Words are communicated out of a need to be heard. Words are spoken and written because of a need to be listened to by an audience of one or many. We talk to each other to express our need, through the Art of Expression, to have *others understand how we feel.* Our deepest desires are resonating at the highest vibration to communicate our Authentic Self.

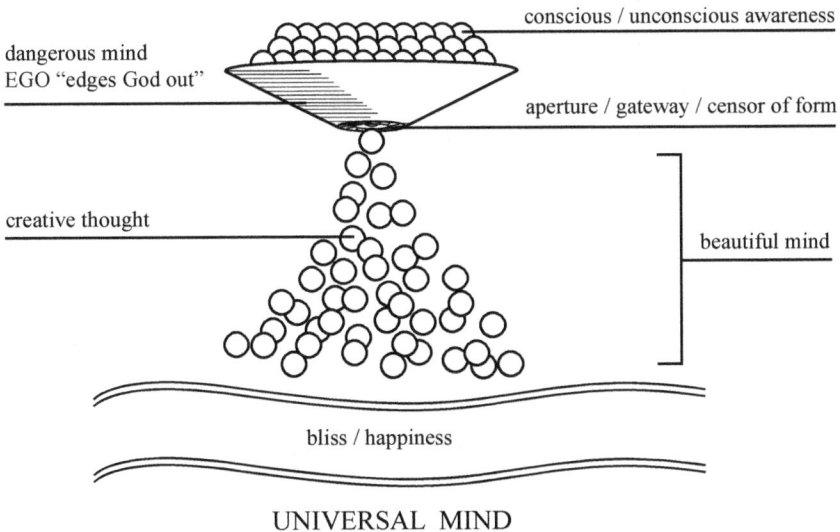

UNIVERSAL MIND

We are not our thoughts, we are the Maker of the thoughts.

3:1

The level of blocks connected to our Conscious /UnConscious Self and our Intuitive Self will determine the degree we are able to express our Self authentically. The weaker the vibration, the less we are able to communicate authenticity creating a stronger attraction to self-doubt. The higher the vibration the clearer the information is expressed without the need to attach discarnate energies. The more we are able to communicate with pure creative expressions without the filter of the emotionally expressed blocks, the clearer the information is expressed. The clearer the expression, the deeper the understanding will be by others of how genuine we are being. How we feel is the gateway to our intuitive level of sensitivity and emotional stability and what we say communicates whether we are being authentic. On a subtler level the world around us is aware of when information conveyed is genuine or not. Every vibration sent out from the mind ripples into the world affecting everything. When the thoughts are connected to feelings they carry a different message intensifying the effect. Being aware of what we think and how we express it is the responsibility of each one of us. It is the difference between thinking and acting from the ego contained personal mind and the universal perfect mind as harmony.

Emotional stability is the connection between our INTUITION (God mind), our HEART (emotional body center) and our WISDOM (abundant freedom).

The Beautiful Mind

The mind is defined as a conscious substratum (foundation) or factor (result producer) in the Universe. The Beautiful Mind is a substance that functions in or promotes the function of a particular physiological process or bodily system in our Beautiful Universe.

The mind is the element, or complex of elements, in an individual that feels, perceives, thinks, wills, and especially reasons. Without the mind the journey of ideas back and forth between Source and expressed Self will not manifest as the human experience.

The Beautiful Mind is the aspect of the Mental-Self that flows from memory to application to manifestation in conjunction with Source. It is the storehouse where we move Expression, fueled by Energy, directed by Intelligence and manifested in Thought to our Highest Vibration of creative consciousness, vision through application and spiritual purpose. The Beautiful Mind is our treasure-mapping processor to create all the ideas, conscious and unconscious connected with intuition, trusting love and infinite abundance planted from the seeds of intention, commitment, and understanding.

The seeds we are _sowing_ are already _knowing_ how they are _growing_ when we stop edging God out!

The memory or recollection gateway through the Mind is our Creativity (the ability to create), the place where profound thoughts surface and float on the Sea of Knowing.

Depending on how deeply connected to unfiltered remembrance of all knowing will determine the level of creativity in expression. If the energy of creativity is blocked, thoughts as ideas will manifest in association with frustration due to not being able to express one's Creative-Self uninhibited. Hence the saying, "frustrated artist!"

When the blocks to the emotional sensitivity of the Emotional-Self challenge the Beautiful Mind as the "frustrated artist," emotional balance cannot collaborate completely with the Inner Soul Child.

The intuitively trusting Abundant-Self is the home of the Inner Soul Child in everyone. The Inner Soul Child is our source of never-ending creativity in laughter, gaiety and play! The Inner Soul Child is the voice beckoning, sometimes screaming at us to take the journey less traveled—though the individualized expression of universal mind. It speaks to us of the adventure unexplored in our daily lives. In ancient times "child" meant of *noble birth*, and today it means, *not yet come of age*. It can perhaps mean *the Ageless-Self, possessing outstanding qualities of expression.* The Ageless-Self is the dominion of our make believe script in our dance of life movie. The Ageless-Self knows the joy of our Self-expression. Like sap expressing itself in the form of a flower, joy in its highest vibration is Bliss. Bliss is defined as complete happiness, paradise or heaven within. The Inner Soul Child desires the journey of joy in everything it is and everything it is not. The Inner Soul Child desires to create our make believe script in our dance of life movie with joy and take all paths to Happiness.

The Inner Soul Child is the most repressed and subjugated voice, speaking to us, in our lives!

What does your Inner Soul Child say to you?

The Beautiful Mind desires to embrace the Inner Child. Yet often the filtering device—self-doubt—censors the voice of the Inner Child. The Beautiful Mind is at the gateway to our Conscious Self and is blocked by the personal memory thoughts (stories) repeated over and over again in the Mental-Self *loop*. The *loop* is comprised of the selected thoughts and stories contained in our beliefs, usually the rational thoughts, which are monitored by self-doubt, intellectual knowledge and restricted beliefs affirming the lack of confidence and distrust in ourselves.

Self-doubt comes from the Dangerous Mind—the aspect of the mind—that believes the road less journeyed is a road full of trepidations and timidity. The Dangerous Mind is where thoughts are collected from falsely interpreted stories (memories) that tell us to be careful, afraid, fearful, and isolated from anything and anyone which might take us out of our rational mind. The Dangerous Mind only collaborates with the Beautiful Mind selectively, and only when convinced that any past fears have been eliminated permanently.

A person who thinks outside of the box is often called mad.

When we allow past or unconscious false memories (stories) to express as self-doubt we will always suppress the Inner Soul Child. Without the Inner Soul Child at play we cannot create new memories or stories that will support creativity. Remember we are making it all up to begin with! The longer we suppress, the harder it is to eliminate all the reinforced censors in our Dangerous Mind and the less we are able to listen to the small little voice of the Inner Soul Child.

It is never too late! All we are required to do is create a deliberate affirmed positive intention to listen to the Inner Soul Child and let it know we are listening by laughing, dancing and playing more! Talking to our Inner Soul Child and listening to what the Inner Soul Child-Self is saying will enable us to tap into deeper levels of joy and happiness.

There are many avenues to take on the journey to the Inner Soul Child and the easiest is to simply decide to allow the Self to *be* in the Beautiful Mind and begin to create dialogue with the Inner Soul Child. Letting go of the *notion* (an individual's conception or impression of something known, experienced, or imagined) or stories of self-doubt can be achieved by recognizing the memories connected to the lower vibrational emotional-Self are false. The memories are only impressions of unhappy moments replayed over and over again that have become distorted by the fabric of time. No matter how much we want to believe they are true, the only fact that can be given are the ones we make believe are true by repeating them over and over again in our mind. If the stories are manifesting as Self-doubt, how is this working for us? If the stories are not connecting with happiness, then we are continually repeating what our impressions of life are to us over and over again with no room left for the stories that allow us to feel good about our Self.

Some may think that taking stories from our past and rewriting and revising them or making them up to feel better about them is a fantasy. I say what choice do we have? Is it not better to first discover the gift in them and then let them go by giving them back to the universe through forgiveness from release or continue to hold on to them and attract the same feelings over and over again?

Once we release and forgive we begin again each day by making choices that serve our *highest and best good.* The first choice is to tell the timid, fear-driven Dangerous Mind that *I am safe!*

Connecting or re-connecting with the Inner Soul Child, with deliberate affirmed positive intentions, will offer an opportunity to begin listening to what the universe is saying to us in regards to joy through Self discovery and exploration of playfulness and laughter.

- *I am bored with me; I'd like to take dance lessons.*
- *I'm tired of complaining about my marriage; we need a romantic vacation.*
- *I'm sick of worrying over bills; I am going to volunteer at a soup kitchen.*
- *I worry too much, like my mother did; I am willing and able to take care of myself.*
- *So I'm not a schooled artist; I am going to start painting for fun.*
- *I'll always have debt—it is part of life, and I'd like to learn the*

piano.
· *I never got to ride a horse when I was little; it is time to take that ride.*
· *All I do is work; I'm joining a bowling league.*
· *We never do anything together; I'm going to plan a picnic.*
· *When is it going to be my turn? How about today?*
· *My mother always complained; I'm not my mother.*
· *My desire to sing is a fantasy; it is time to make it a reality.*
· *When I was a little boy I loved trains; it is time for a train set!*
· *I loved dressing up like a princess; I'm going to have a costume party.*

The Art of Expression is not in a fantasy mind, but in the Beautiful Mind. It is easy to believe that the things we truly desire in our life we may never create. This is false. The truth is the only expression desired is to lose ambiguity about *who we really are* and to connect from the outer world to our inner world. Attaining a collaboration of the Intuitive-Self and the Beautiful Mind, the misconceptions have to stop regarding *who I am* and begin to align the Authentic Self, with deliberate affirmed positive intentions, to create clarity. This is not done by appraising the pros and cons of an idea to death in the analytical process but through meditation and listening to the first answer that is received. It is a state of asking the universe to give us the one creative idea that will embark us on the path of the road less traveled to higher consciousness and happiness. When we have the bright Light of Self Love—merging with Trust in Intuition and the Abundant Wisdom from listening to the inner voice of the Soul Child within—the abundant creativity in emotional Self-expression will take flight liberating each of us into the One-Self. The Authentic Self is planting seeds of intentions to express the One-Self, unblocked, on the journey less traveled. This connection will expand our Trust in our Self through new dialogue not imbedded with Self-doubt in the false memory multifaceted-Self.

The Dangerous Mind will recede and be replaced by the Beautiful Mind allowing us to expand and express our deepest desire to be authentic in our *words* and *deeds*.

In a world where what we say and what we mean can forever be united, the first step is to listen to voice from our Inner Soul Child's shout of laughter and joy! From this deeper pool we begin to communicate words to each other and express desires for everyone to know what it is to be happy—recognized as the ever-constant liquid truth centered in the Authentic Self. Then, and only then, will we believe that our Beautiful Mind is the aspect of our Authentic Self tapping into the Universal Mind, or God.

The Authentic Self

In the everyday life the notion of living an authentic life appears impossible. The world reflects multifaceted images to us. For example, the demanding role to act in a certain manner with different faces begins when we are very young. We are taught to perform in many diverse roles. As children we are taught right from wrong, good from bad, and how we are expected to act according to the codes of the community. From our parents we quickly learn what responses will get us what we want in life. In school we are expected to act within a certain protocol with teachers and other students. At play we are expected to behave and participate within the peer group. Everywhere and every day we learn what face to wear in which situation. The roles we play in our make believe life movie become second nature as we grow up and develop craftiness discovering what works for us and what doesn't work very well.

Every moment is strategically honed to reinforce our need to be accepted with each group we are invited to join. We learn to conveniently lie on cue to cover any feelings of inadequacy and cover up painful lessons that have been reinforced in our experiences. No one wants to feel or act stupid. No one desires to be unloved or unwanted. No one wants to be unacceptable. Every moment is guided by a need to be part of something else. So we lie, we conceal, we deny, and we comply in order to find approval.

Eventually we find the faces that will serve us the best and accommodate us to whatever situation each face is best suited. We discover that, indeed, we are great actors and actresses. We are able to flow into any character required to facilitate whatever scenario is scripted. Our ability to be multifaceted is measured in how well we are able to become whatever role is necessary at any given moment in the day.

There is a need to please everyone with the minimum level of conflict (resistance) and the emotional-sensitive desire to have others feel good about us. It is the "people pleaser" in everyone living a multifaceted life.

Since we have been living this way as far back as we remember we believe it is our natural internal nature. Everyone around us is living the same multifaceted life and getting along, *right?*

By the time we are adults we have taken ownership of who we think we are. We believe we have connected to *Who I Am*. What we have done is connected to a false sense of true identity.

· *I am a mother and a wife and a sister and a banker.*
· *I am a brother and a football player and a social worker.*
· *I am a preacher and a teacher and a dancer.*
· *I am a student and a lesbian and a waitress.*

· *I am a player and married and a tax consultant.*

❖ **How many faces do you have?**

Our multifaceted Self is divided into as many people pleasers as necessary to create the least amount of conflict (resistance) in each day of life.

The Conscious Self processes as many different aspects of the Self as we believe our identity incorporates at any given time. No wonder we are exhausted by the end of each day!

The level of energy necessary to generate such an amount of diversity in action is enormous! Every day the process begins the moment we wake up and start the new day.

The inAuthentic Self is in command. We become comfortably numb and expect nothing to change. The journey becomes the path of least resistance or living below the radar.

Living below the radar is simply the deliberate negatively affirmed intention to go unnoticed and seen as not unique and different. It is the desire to move through life with the least amount of resistance on the journey.

When the resistance is obvious it is usually due to some glitch in the day created by an inner conflict. If the inner conflict gets too bottled up, we take a stand. And when we stand, at this point we rise above the radar detector and an alarm goes off allowing everyone who has been ignoring us to notice a different behavioral pattern. Depending on how long we can handle the resistance of being above the radar will determine how connected we are to our uniqueness. Being unique has the modern qualifier that defines those living above the radar as being peculiar.

And who wants to be thought of as behaving or acting peculiar?
The word "unique" historically meant *that which is like nothing*

else in comparison. Unique is that which stands out.

Being unique is not in balance with the status quo. Being unique is living above the radar!

The Authentic Self is unique.

In the deepest expression of the emotional-Self we may feel there must be more to life than the life we are living. In the Art of Expression creativity is swelling up from the Source desiring to have others know *who I really am* and understanding *how I really feel.* There is a deep desire to break free of self-doubt and the needs of others' expectations and become the Authentic Self within God.

But all blocks created from fear is the Dangerous Mind telling us not to do it! If we begin to allow our Self to say what we really feel and live the life we really wish for, what happens to the life we are living now? The life we have created out of a lifetime of being inauthentic will change dramatically and there may be consequences.

What the inAuthentic Self is not telling us is the "consequences" are worse if we continue living the life we participate in now. The inner conflicts will only be bottled and the pressure of continuing to bottle up true feelings will lead to emotional blocks that can manifest in cancer, ulcers, nervous disorders, alcoholism, drug dependencies, *dis*-illusionment, or a combination of all of the *dis*-eases now common in life. The inAuthentic Self never reminds us to stop saying what we don't mean and start speaking potential truth based on a desire to have people really know *who I really am*—accepting, honoring and loving us for who we are.

The path to authenticity is the path least walked. It is full of change, new dialogues, and unique adventures. The path to authenticity is the road to discovering the Self we may have yet to meet.

The Dangerous Mind always warns us of any new paths because they are highways into uncharted territory. All uncharted territory is unsafe to the Dangerous Mind!

The Authentic Self is unwavering and connotes definite origin from Source.

It never creates from a place of unconsciousness by being:

Condescending
Malicious
Multi-faced
Pretentious
False
Negative
Fake
Untrustworthy
Opinionated
Gossipy
Judgmental
Pacifying
Resentful

The Authentic Self flows from the Creative Source and is:

Trustworthy
Open and Willing To Change
Truthful
Compassionate
Affirmative
Fair
Judicial
Understanding

Responsible to Itself
For the Best and Highest Good

The Authentic Self is in cooperation with the Beautiful Mind, allowing Abundance and knowing Wisdom is not multi-faceted but resides in integrity from Truth expressed through the Conscious-Self.

ʃ ʃ ʃ

Imagine a machine in your house you can program every day to design whatever you want to wear. Standing in the machine it dresses you in new attire. All the materials, colors and the design are suited to your individual taste and are not dependent on how anyone else is dressed. You go to work, school or the store wearing on your body what illuminates your unique creative Self.

What kind and style of clothes will you wear?

Imagine yourself attracting the kind of relationship you want—by becoming the lover in yourself you desire in someone else.

What kind of lover will you create?

Imagine the place you will live if you have all the money in the world.

Where will you live?

Imagine being able to be authentic in Conscious Self all the time without having to behave the way other people think you should.

Who will you be?

With all the faces you have in your week, take a look at each one of them separately and write down the attributes that allow you to feel good about that person within. Then write down all the attributes of the different faces you play in your daily life which *do not* allow you to feel good about yourself. Look at both lists carefully and see who all these people collectively represent. Some of the attributes will be aspects of your parents, people you admire, heroes, women, men, and friends. The characteristics are from both the behavior of people you have honored and people you have disliked. All the characteristics are aspects of your multi-faceted Self.

After careful examination of the positive and negative characteristics and behavior, ask yourself why you chose, through deliberate affirmed positive and negative intentions, to mirror what is not authentic in who you are?

I am a woman in a corporate man's world; I have to act like them.
· *My boss makes me cater to him; I feel like a slave.*
· *Sex with my husband is boring, so I would rather gain weight.*
· *I married to have children, not because I love my spouse.*
· *I hate my job, but I am too old to start over.*
· *I never say what I mean; I am always misunderstood.*
· *If I said what I really felt, people would not like me.*
· *My boss is a jerk; I act like I like him.*
· *I hide my feelings because it is polite.*
· *I never take candy from a stranger.*
· *I smile to hide my unhappiness.*
· *I don't always tell the truth because it gets me in trouble.*
· *I look outside myself for love, to know how love feels.*

Now look at the list of attributes you like about yourself. The way you act that allows you to feel good about yourself.

· *I am trustworthy.*
· *I speak honestly when I am asked my feelings about something.*
· *I am understanding.*
· *I believe other people's opinions of me are none of my business.*
· *I treat everybody fairly.*
· *I love my career and work to make a difference.*
· *I follow the road less journeyed.*
· *I don't harbor resentments.*
· *I am honest in my relationships with others.*
· *I believe people do not require my approval.*
· *I see only the divine Light in everybody.*
· *I accept people for who they are.*
· *I do not spread rumors through gossip.*
· *Opinions are none of my business.*

After examining the aspects of yourself you no longer want to emulate, write the statements in reverse as higher vibrations. For example, instead of, "*If I said what I really felt, people would not like me,*" you can say, "*If I really say what I feel, from a place of love, I will be honoring my Higher-Self.*"

Next write down all the aspects that are revealed on another sheet of paper. Take a look at what choices you are now intending to create, and say them out loud to yourself. Feel the higher vibration of these positive affirmed thoughts that feel good as words.

Circle the choices that you desire to sustain in your daily life. Look at the intentions as *Who I Am* and merge them into your

Beautiful Mind. Embrace the thoughts as your new positive affirmed intentions (affirmations), saying to yourself, *"This is who I really am!"*

Repeat to your Self different affirmations every day. Pick the ones which best apply to each situation, always holding the intention, *"I am affirming my Authentic Self!"*

ဪ ဪ ဪ

The gateway to the Conscious Self is being sensitive to all feelings from the Source of Being and collaborating with those feelings (intuition/heart-center/wisdom). The more the thoughts are allowed to flow freely through emotional stability, the greater the feelings expressed from integrity. The Heart represents our ability to trust what we feel—the intuitive vibration, which allows the Conscious Self to free our conscious gateway of information (thoughts). In other words, the more we are able to trust in what we intuitively sense is coming from the Authentic Self, the more we receive clearer information from Source. This is where connection to ESP and psychic Self (the Self that perceives nonphysical or supernatural forces and influences marked by extraordinary or mysterious sensitivity, or understanding) exists.

The profounder the trust in our deepest feelings, the clearer the psychic Self communicates through our Authentic Beautiful Mind. This enables the connection to the Authentic Self to blossom into feelings which tap into our free Self, a vibration the heart-center yearns to express.

With deliberate affirmed positive intentions, and daily practice, our Beautiful Mind will think from our deepest expressions.

Dialogue and Sensitivity

Recognizing the potential of our Authentic Self also requires an awareness of perceived and spoken dialogue. The thoughts we choose and how we express our words into action are usually how others will know what we feel. Many times what is said is not what is meant; and how we say it is connected strategically to a comfortable vocabulary.

The memories we carry are not connected directly to Words. Memories are images connected together in our minds to make *scenarios* edited into stories we apply to our movie. The finished movie is what we remember of the experience. It is never actually the real event. Memories are *seen* rather than *described*. Each scenario connects to feelings every time they are *re*-remembered. The farther away the event horizon, the less detail is remembered.

Sometimes the memories are simply diluted, forgotten in the Conscious-Self, forever stored in the deeper vaults of the Mind, but faded memories have *residual response feelings or programs attached.*

Sensitivity—awareness of the needs and emotions of others—is required in the process of communicating feelings. Dialogue connected to our emotional-sensitive Self is received in the manner it is spoken, and the perception filters of the people we are talking to will decipher what we are *feeling* about what we are *saying*. The dynamic interplay is understood by how each person is connected to all the scenarios in their re-remembered "residual response feelings" or programs. They also are filtering the dialogue with sensitivity—awareness of the needs and emotions of *us*—to interpret feelings.

Back and forth the dialogue will play until the messages are confirmed and accepted or resisted. The resisted dialogue will create responses attached to inner conflicts and will often trigger responses which mirror our *inner conflicts.* Remember, inner conflicts are created from unresolved feelings and are connected to beliefs that are not in alignment with desires.

Since dialogue plays such an enormous role in *who I am* and *how I feel*, the dialogues we have are usually scripts that have been used over and over again. They are cultivated from past emotional-sensitive scenarios that we know have worked for us in the past, at least to some degree. Rarely is there a need to alter the scenarios unless the Dangerous Mind is fearful the outcome will cause us to go above the radar, forcing us to create *outside* our comfort zone. The Dangerous Mind will suggest it is better to justify your behavior than to admit there might be a different opportunity to understand. The Dangerous Mind will tell us to stick to what we know, even if it is causing us to have inner conflicts, because how we feel is how we have *always felt.*

And what is wrong with that? At least we know how that feels!

It is difficult to view an inner conflict as a Gift. How are the feelings we have always felt ever going to change? *How can inner conflicts be a Gift?*

The Gift is in how we express our inner conflicts through the dialogue we choose with everyone. Whether you know it or not, everyone can sense how we really feel. It is the most fascinating and beautiful thing about who we really are. Everyone can sense everyone else's inner conflicts because everyone has inner conflicts!

The Gift is the *mirror.* Instead of understanding our inner conflicts, we will become involved in helping others to understand their inner conflicts. It somehow seems easier. The Gift is every time we become involved in their inner conflicts we are magnifying our own struggles. The amount of our ability to "help" someone else will determine how much we are willing to "help" our Self. At some point either the inner conflict is balanced with desire equaling belief, or the personal struggles become so resistant that we, them or both of us will move away from the vibrations because the resistance is too intense only to address the same issues or inner conflicts with perhaps someone else.

When the need to resolve our inner conflicts equals the desire to have our beliefs in alignment with our deepest desires, the opportunity for new dialogue will be created. This alignment will be created because of our openness to be willing to change and allow the growth in conscious awareness.

It is important to recognize the dialogues that are not working for us. Not by focusing on them but perhaps by simply seeing the opportunity to change them. Whatever feelings are brought to the surface in our Self is how we feel about ourselves and it may have nothing to do with the buttons being pushed by another. The inner emotional conflicts within are ours and ours alone to understand. We must simply understand the emotional button(s) being pushed in us should not be taken as a personal affront. The issues and conflicts are not theirs but our own. It is wiser to simply bless them and thank them for continually pushing those buttons so we can remain aware there are still parts of our Self we have not healed. When those aspects are healed the buttons will simply vanish! We shall salute the button pushers in all of us as how we are receiving the gifts necessary to change. But unfortunately and often times, we are in victim mode and the "button pusher" becomes the object of disdain instead of looking within to see where and what it is the inner conflict within. Instead, we simply point the finger back at them and become the accuser examining the motive of the person who is pushing the buttons. The button is attached to express the need to begin an inner search for why there is a button in the first place.

Everyone is aware of what these scripted dialogues are in their daily lives. They are the ones we are having every time we have an argument about finances, the kids, the college buddy, the ex-girlfriend, the next door neighbor, the best friend, the boss, the drinking buddies, the mother-in-law or who should do the dishes!

❖ **What dialogues do you repeat in your daily life?**

Take a look at the dialogues which reflect inner conflict with an outer appearance of the button pusher and begin to understand why they are not serving your best and highest good. We are required to examine the scenarios and why they are connected to our inner conflicts, remembering that inner conflicts are directly connected to beliefs that are not in alignment with our deepest desires. It is always important to take another look in our *God box* and see how the inner conflicts are connected to the beliefs we are still refusing to let go. It is always important to re-examine our beliefs.

ॐ ॐ ॐ

Again ask yourself,

Do they allow me to feel good about others and myself?

Once you have taken a thorough look at the inner conflicts that are unresolved, allow your Self to feel gratitude to all the people in your life who reflect what you desire to appreciate and understand. Then begin each day to see how you can change the dialogues you are having with others and yourself. The inner dialogues that are not allowing you to feel good about your Self are the personal Gifts to your Self. Allow them to surface and embrace them fully within your Self. Know they are yours and not anyone else's. You have created them out of all your re-remembered scenarios played over and over again. Know they are only what you remember, not the reality they once held the day you experienced them. The only reality you are having is today. Yesterday is only a memory (re-remembered with residual feelings and false images), and tomorrow is only a desire wanting to be fulfilled once you throw out the garbage that is taking up room in your mind.

How do you feel about today?

Another opportunity for connecting with the dialogues that are manifesting lower vibrational feelings and interpreted by the mind as negative affirmed thoughts is to let the person who is mirroring your inner conflicts know that it is time to change the dialogue that you are both having with each other!

At first the other person may seem confused by your statement, but the truth is they will probably agree. If the dialogue is not serving either of you, then it will resonate with the other party too. It is dialogue that you both can agree to change for the highest good in both of you. The other person is feeling the lower vibration, or negative affirmed thoughts as well and they may be tired of repeating the same scenario that ends in the same way each time also.

Let the other person know you understand the dialogue continues to go nowhere and it is creating bad feelings about yourselves. Tell them the only reason you continue to use the words you say is because having not yet discovered a better way to communicate with them, and with their help and collaboration, both of you can remind each other when the loop starts and ends the same way. One or both of you can choose to stop the dialogue until a dialogue that allows you both to feel good about what needs to be communicated is created.

Furthermore, provide an explanation for the same responses and challenges by saying it is because of your own personal inner conflict on the matter. If you know what the belief is that is creating the inner conflict, explain what the conflict is within your Self. If you are still not sure, then explain to them you are searching in your beliefs for the reasons behind the dialogue. But also inform them the inner conflicts are not allowing you to feel good about your Self and are, therefore, not allowing them to feel good about you or more importantly their Self. Tell them it is nothing personal and explain the dialogues you are having with other people are no better. Let the person know that you cannot see their Divine Light any better than you can see your own.

𝕾 𝕾 𝕾

Always remember, we can only treat others as well as we treat ourselves no matter what we believe about the matter. We might believe we are treating them better, but they are probably aware enough to understand how little we really love our Self.

· *I am the Divine Light within me.*
· *I love others for exactly who they are.*
· *It is nothing personal.*
· *My inner conflicts can be understood.*
· *I am choosing to change my dialogues to feel good.*
· *I am open and willing to change.*
· *I allow others to grow and I allow myself the same privilege.*

Creative Sensitivity

Expression is fueled by Energy, directed by Intelligence and manifested in Thought. This experience is called creative sensitivity.

It is who we are in our Perfect Self whether we know it or not. The beauty of this process-in-progress is perfect and divine. The perfection is the Truth that we are all able to express ourselves at our highest vibrations, and we are all going to eventually know the truth whether we believe it or not. We can allow the creative process or we can resist it. However if we choose to make the journey, we will all arrive into our highest vibration of our Creative Divine Light safe and sound.

In our Creative Divine Light we are co-creating with the original Light, with the All as is suggested by the statement, "In the beginning..." As we observe when we look at nature there is creativity expressing itself in all things. Looking in the mirror, we gaze upon our own relevant creation awe struck by the intricacy of design. In everything creativity is sensitive, capable of indicating minute differences, subtle and sublime, in the expression of Energy, directed by Intelligence and manifested in Thought.

We are the expression of Energy, directed by Intelligence and manifested in Thought. We are Perfect Creative Sensitivity manifesting!

Discovery

1. How many faces do you have?

2. **Choose different affirmations every day to repeat to your Self. Pick the affirmations that best apply to your different daily situations, always holding the positive affirmed intention, "I am becoming my Authentic Self!"**

3. **What dialogues do you repeat in your daily life? Every time you begin to play an inner dialogue that is familiar, take a moment and write it down in the most detail you can. Most people have four or five dialogues they play over and over again in their head or often repeat out loud to others. See if you can recognize them when they arise. Examine the dialogues and see where they might have developed and why they cause so much frustration in your life.**

After you have written them all down, give them each a name. Each time one of them appears say the name of it out loud and then laugh. Say to your Self, "This is the old me. I am not that person anymore. I have replaced that old dialogue with positive affirmed thoughts today."

Everyday Affirmations

I am trustworthy.
I speak honestly when I am asked my feelings about something.
I am connected to the creative source within.
I believe other people's opinions of me are none of my business.
I treat everybody equally and with respect.

I love my career and work to make a difference.

I follow the road less journeyed.

I have let go of all resentments.

I am honest in my relationships with others.

I believe people do not require my approval.

I see only the Divine Light in everybody.

I accept people for who they are.

Do what you can, with what you have, where you are.

- Henry David Thoreau

Chapter 4

Foundations and Commitment

The Will

There are two types of Will.

The first is a habitual action or natural tendency that is done almost unconsciously. This is called our comfort zone, and it is the will we use most often in our day. It is thoughts we hold during our daily life routine. This comfort zone is in repetition and becomes the unconscious actions we plan and count on throughout our lives. The beliefs we hold to be truth creates our perception of reality, and because it is a reality born of our own made up creation, we can be resistant to change. Yet, beliefs are only a collection of thoughts that we willingly hold together.

Changes occur in our lives when the beliefs we hold on to no longer connect to new desires. Such an opportunity to change may appear as an obstacle if we willingly resist the change. The amount of resistance to change deepens the teachings presented to us and are further revealed as we open to the allowing of new and different thoughts that form into new beliefs.

The second type of will is the Divine Will, which vibrates from our Higher Conscious Self, the All Knowing, God/Goddess, Universal Life Force and the Enlightened Self. This place within us is where That-Which-Is-In-Divine-Order and For-Highest-and-Best-Good resonates oftentimes as the vibrations that are outside our comfort zone. The road less chosen often appears scary and new. Yet, this is the path, which allows us to release our control over the outcome of expectations. The path of least resistance can be tempered in the belief that "everything is alright in my world" and "I am safe" to create more perfect balance. This is the opportunity to recognize what is the balance in both having human will and being an aspect of the Divine Will.

Where is your Will today?

Stability

In the center of each individualized Self is the domain of the dynamic physical Will, the place where the foundation of being human is steady of purpose and firm in resolution. It is the abode where the rooted Self is watered, fed and nurtured to embrace Love in Divine application. It is the dominion where seeds are planted and are emotionally expressed, through creative Thought, to be patiently rooted, eventually realizing purpose. Without this dominion nothing will grow tall enough to stand empowered. Stability is only achieved when an enduring foundation is created: solid, firm and strong. It is the rock we build everything on, grounding the heart from the will (the power of intention) of the Conscious-Self.

On the physical plane it is the very Earth we stand upon, the very ground where all possible expression becomes manifested. This is where seeds of intention are sown and patiently nurtured to understand the inner process that leads to the mystery of All things in motion through the step-by-step process of growth and development.

It is the fixed nature only in the absolute unchanging Higher Consciousness bringing all things into equilibrium through motion, allowing stability to be sustained. It is where intention, intuition and creative expression can become steadfast and certain. It is the very rock we build our church—human being as the temple of Heaven on Earth.

Stability reduces the constant strain of stress, pressure, and uncertainty in everything.

The Conscious Self channels through the mind the creative thought (information) which will then determine how thought may be applied. But the mind is only a thinking machine and unable to manifest without the step-by-step process required in the formulation. Without stability in action what dreams can be strengthened? The dreams remain only dreams and never take root in firmness from solid building. No skyscraper will be realized without a solid foundation and will remain forever in the form of architectural drawings. To build the building it is required to understand how important the underlayment is in the process.

It sounds logical and practical. Yet how many times have we started something with the intention of seeing it manifested and somewhere along the way we gave up because of impatience or by simply deciding to skip a step in the process? How many times did our dreams become unstable and tumble down and thus become unrealized?

Connecting to the Process

The process is a series of actions or operations that contribute to desirable results. In order to build anything, it is important to understand the stages of development to achieve the outcome.

Often times it becomes the most difficult aspect of the task or achievement. If the knowledge of what is required to develop or build is not understood, then the process becomes more about OJT, *on-the-job training.* OJT is more about learning as we go than understanding what we are RTK, *required to know.* OJT is what happens when information is unavailable from the Conscious Self. It also happens when communication is not allocated.

This lack of communication creates the opportunities to make poor decisions. The RTK is undermined, and ultimately any development will become unstable in the undertaking. The lack of knowledge of which building blocks are required becomes the *doom-before-you-begin* motto.

Self discovery is found in the art of clarity and is required in determining how willing we are to listen to the information and process it through a willingness to clarify, commit and have patient endurance with completing the goal. Feeling good about our seeds of intention and the clarity of information expressed will allow a plan to take shape. Taking the plan and gathering the tools with what you are required to know (RTK), will allow you to trust the outcome. This is the *process* for applying, understanding and connecting to the wisdom of what we manifest to purpose.

Understanding the stages of development is accepting that one of the important stages is *patience.*

Patience is being steadfast despite opposition, adversity or difficulty! It is a main ingredient in any process. And patience is lenient—the mild and stress-free calmness associated with one of many aspects of Love.

How many times has acting impatient created stress in our life? How many steps have been overlooked in the stages of developing and manifesting certain desires? Patience is often one of the most overlooked aspects of the creative process in motion. Patience is connected to the long run (time and practice) and our ability to have all the necessary tools—specifically endurance, permanence, and most importantly, balanced inner and outer strength to succeed. It is the marathon manifested!

Patience is the ingredient allowing us to take every step without stress caused by being too rigid and having fixed ideas about the goal. Behind every great intention expressed there is the ability for all creativity in motion to manifest from a place of patience during the process.

Not being hasty or impetuous in believing that the road less traveled is determined by the shortest road is key, as well as understanding that all the proper ingredients are necessary to make the perfect soufflé! Process takes time and practice.

This is just like the process of making a movie. First we start with an idea and then we write the script. The quality of the script is governed by how able we are to listen to the expression from within the creative process. If the movie can be made, because all the ingredients are present, the next level is to decide whether or not it is cost effective and can be made within a certain budget. If we have a working budget, then it is time to plan out what we need to provide in order to shoot the project. From cameras to sets, actors to a music score, every detail is listed and formulated within the necessary budget. Once all the elements are in place, and only when every "T" is crossed, is the pre-production complete. Everything and everybody is in place. Now it is time to set the goal of how long it will take to complete the filming. A schedule is created for every day of every shot. And when the day comes to start shooting, it is ready, set, action! From that moment forward every event is monitored to make sure that the movie is on schedule, because if it isn't, it will go over budget and actors and crew who have committed to the project may not be available. It is made with the intention of finishing on time. And the process of making a movie is getting through all the obstacles and events that show up during the filming with as little resistance as possible. It depends on fortitude, endurance and patience to see it through to the end. And even when the filming is completed, there are still more post-production aspects that must be attended to.

It sounds so rigid and fixed. However, the process of making a movie is fluid and creative. Every day it is imperative to be flexible and make allowances for things that do not work or may be over-worked. It takes an ability to make flash decisions, which may not have been present before. For example, we may have to shift scenes to another day because an actor is ill or there has been an accident on set, or a myriad of other obstacles that can happen. It is a very creative and flexible journey that is fixed within a budget and a schedule.

Making a movie is very much the same thing we are doing while we are making the movie called *My Life on the G-list*! The "G" is for God.

The only difference may be in the professionalism. Everybody involved in making a movie is willing to collaborate with the process. They know that each piece is required to complete the puzzle. *It is a practical process.*

Making movies is a creative process that takes time and practice. It is also an emotionally charged process that is both personal and sensitive to all the aspects that are required.

Sometimes the process exceeds the practicality and the movie is scrapped costing a lot of wasted time and energy; usually because all the pieces were not processed in accordance with the desired results.

When taking the first step in realizing what it is we intend to do, it is important to spend the time to figure out how it will be done. The planning phase is where we begin to root our ideas into the ground.

Once the roots are allowed to mature, there is the flowering process that bears fruit and not a moment before.

Then why is it most of the time we are in so much of a hurry? What appears to be the rush?

Usually the rush, which is impatience, manifests because the planning stage was either not well thought out or we are going by the skin of our teeth. If the planning stage is not given time to be formulated in a way that allows us to feel good about the foundation, then it is time to look at what perhaps might be our fear of success.

A fear of success is expressed in instability. *Being stable is a deliberate intention connected to commitment.* Being committed is reflected in relationships, homes and work. When any one of these aspects become about commitment, stability will be in motion. If, there is instability, inner conflicts will upset the balance. The lack of balance will cause inner stability to be under scrutiny emotionally, physically and mentally. Every commitment is mirrored in how well the foundations are built in family, education and physical activity. If at any level the underlying feelings are not in alignment with the outcome, then the foundation will appear suspect. When we feel we are unable to succeed in our desires, the best place to look is inside our Self.

❖ **Take a look at your relationships.**

· *What is the inner conflict I have about relationships?*
· *Why is the commitment so difficult?*
· *What were my experiences that have inhibited me from allowing myself long-lasting relationships which reflect who I desire to become?*
· *Why are my relationships unsuccessful?*
· *What kind of relationship did my parents have with each other?*
· *Where did I learn about relationships?*

126

· *How are the relationships of my friends?*
· *What do their relationships reflect on my own?*
· *Is my present relationship successful?*
· *What are my expectations in relationships?*
· *When did I turn into my parents?*
· *Why don't I have an honest relationship?*

❖ **Take a look at your job.**

· *Why don't I love my job?*
· *What is preventing me from doing the best job I can?*
· *Why do I jump from job to job?*
· *Why do I do the work I do?*
· *Why didn't I follow my dreams?*
· *What is preventing me now from finding my dream job?*
· *Where is the Joy in work?*
· *Why is work so hard?*
· *Why don't I believe the saying "If you love what you do, the money will come?"*
· *Why does it appear other people are more successful than I am?*
· *Why am I stuck in my career?*

❖ **Take a look at your education.**

· *What do I need to learn to get what I want?*
· *Why do I feel so stupid?*
· *What will it take to get what I want?*
· *Why don't I take art or music classes?*
· *What will it take for me to feel smart enough?*
· *Why do I think higher education is only from higher learning?*

· *When is it going to be my turn?*
· *What did my parents think of education?*
· *What did I want to learn in school that they didn't teach me?*
· *What did I love in school that I could learn more about?*
· *What did I teach my children about education that isn't true?*

❖ **Take a look at your physical activities.**

· *Did my parents play with me?*
· *Are sports important to my family?*
· *What prevents me from participating in recreational activities?*
· *Why do I not work out regularly?*
· *What is important about my body?*
· *Why don't I take care of my body?*
· *Why don't I have any self-discipline?*
· *Am I flexible?*
· *Is a flexible body connected to a flexible outlook on life?*
· *Do I take care of my body?*
· *How easy is it to beat myself up?*
· *Do I bruise easily?*

❖ **What commitments are you afraid to make?**

Physical, emotional and mental stability are the first steps in attaining our higher goals in life. Connecting to physical stability is finding the balance on the physical plane. When we are not connected, the lessons of inequalities, from the lack of physical stability, are played over and over again until balance is restored or renewed. The physical lessons are reflected in how we connect to our beliefs in the God box. The more our beliefs are in alignment with our desires, the greater the stability.

· *If I don't work hard, I won't make any money.*
· *I put everything important to me off to the last minute.*
· *I want to be organized but I feel overwhelmed.*
· *I think life should be easy; why is it so hard?*

Maybe you are too fixed in your ideas?

· *Money comes easily to me. I work smarter.*
· *I prioritize everything by importance first.*
· *I am as organized as I wish to be.*
· *Life is hard. Now that I know this it seems easier.*

Getting Out of Your Own Way

The process of deciding is a determination arrived at after the consideration. All decisions are grounded in the firmness of conclusion. It is just a matter of getting out of our own way. However, the getting-out-of-the-way process often is the hardest aspect. It is usually about getting unstuck first!

Arriving at a conclusion, making the decision or standing on firm ground is created more effortlessly after carefully weighing the pros and cons. The entire decision-making process is determined by looking at all the intentions energetically; in other words, patiently considering all the opportunities on both sides. Whenever there is an opportunity for one thing, there is the counter-balance of a missed opportunity on the other side. Understanding what both sides have to offer, respectively, is the perfect opportunity to take a deeper look at how we feel about each one in determining the outcome for our best and highest good.

Getting out of our way is the process of finding the balance between the Conscious Self and the Emotional-Self. *In matters of the heart we already know how we feel about all the aspects of the decision.* Our heart tells us there can be only one decision based on trust and love. The inner conflict is between what the personal mind over- or under- analyzes. The Beautiful Mind will connect to the feelings from the heart-center and intuition recognizing the higher vibration of truth to arrive at a decision. The Dangerous Mind will bounce back and forth between all the pros and cons over and over again in a loop, continuously weighing all the possible outcomes and results of each scenario, never wanting to make any commitment. The Dangerous Mind will get stuck in a data loop unable to connect to the Heart for backup! The Heart is not allowed to connect to the decision-making process because both aspects of the Self are not grounded. So the loop continues to feed back on itself until amplified into frustration.

Stuck, from being in our own way, is the process of disconnecting from our Divine Will; it is the *loop of confusion.* It happens when we turn away from our Light and decide the Dangerous Mind can figure it out without any help from the Authentic Self. Deciding on how deep into darkness we choose to journey is determined by how unstable our foundation is. The instability of the foundation is because of emotionally based abandonment or betrayal issues from the past, which are currently manifested as feeling unprotected and unsafe.

The feeling of lacking support can range from emotional to financial, and all the aspects in between. The past feelings connected to the memories of lacking support will become the scenarios that loop again and again, agitating the process necessary to Trust our emotional responses associated with making sound decisions.

The past is not who we are today.

The past is only the journey so far. It is a collection of stored memories, or stories we continually re-remember—since they are no longer real. They are no longer personal experiences except how we feel about them. Today is the only personal experience we are having!

The value placed on how we were treated, how we were raised and what lessons we have learned is only there to remind us there are many opportunities to explore more unique experiences in life. The past is selected stories we identify with, and not the present or the future. Confusion and conflict will manifest when we are unable to reconcile the feelings we have about past negative affirmed stories and the new positive affirmed thoughts presented to us today. Understanding why we feel misunderstood or alone to figure it all out on our own opens a doorway to committing to the small voice inside which guides us. Then we are not divided by the loops our Dangerous Mind replays.

· *The Universe within supports me.*
· *I am safe to decide the best course of action.*
· *I trust in the decisions I make.*
· *I reconcile the pros and cons in my mind and I trust my deeper feelings.*
· *I release my past stories and know all is well in my world.*
· *I stand firmly and securely in right action.*

Standing Still

In a world of super-achievers and application experts, the need for destination depends on how reliable our information is at the time. It is also dependent on the commitment to manifesting the concept in the step-by-step planning process and the decision to create based on understanding the pros and cons and the better opportunity.

The world is making decisions every day. Each of us is making decisions as well. We are making decisions, whether we feel supported or not, and the outcome will reflect the lessons. It is the decision-making process.

We are traveling along our journey, learning lessons, making decisions, manifesting outcomes and the world turns. But one day while traveling the road and believing we are paying attention, we slam head-on into a brick wall. *What happened? I know I am no longer stuck? I figured out what to do. Why is this wall in front of me?*

Taking a step back, with the bump on our head, we look around to see what to do next. After surveying the wall and observing how high it is, how wide it is, and how thick it appears to be, we scratch our heads and begin to ponder what to do next. Looking around we calculate the equipment necessary to bulldoze it down—or go though it—and at the emotional, financial and/or physical cost it will take. Then we consider how long it will take to get around it. How long will we be sidetracked on our journey? We wonder if it is possible to climb over it. How tall of a tower or ladder must we erect to get to the other side? But then how will we get down the other side without falling and hurting our Self? The endeavor appears more complex than previously thought. *So now what?*

The Determined Self may believe the only way to get to the other side is to do whatever it takes. *The Will can be exerted to accomplish the task.* Whatever the struggle, the outcome is worth it!

The outcome is everything. All we have worked for and everything we have accomplished has led, once again, to this very moment! We believe we have planned well and our execution has been flawless, up until now.

The outcome is our destiny, because we are *destiny-driven!* All we can see is where we wish to be. Everything depends on it. Everything.

Yet there is the wall—the wall that is temporarily in our path, the wall we must get through. The wall is what we become *fixed* upon in wonder and frustration.

Never think for a moment that the wall has been placed in front of us to shut us down.

The wall is not in front of us to prevent us from going anywhere. It is in front of us to allow us to stand still. It is there to ask us to listen. It is in front of us to tell us that the road we are taking is not the road we really want to travel any longer. We have had it our way because we think *I want it,* but the truth is we have never felt good. Our deeper feelings have never felt good about the journey we are taking and now it is time to listen. The Authentic Self, our Inner Soul Child, has finally had enough!

We can scream and shout all we want, and the tantrum can go on for a long time in some instances, but we know it is what we have been longing for, forever. Part of us has given up hoping we will ever have what we want. That is the same part that convinced us of our unworthiness to receive any such Gifts. But the wall, the enormous obstacle we are facing, is offering us a unique opportunity. The Unique Self is suggesting that this time the road less traveled is not a road at all. It is time to re-assess and re-evaluate what it is we re-remember about why we are taking this path in the first place.

The highest vibration for our journey is telling us to just stand still and listen.

It is simply a time to stand still, take in all that has led us to this moment, and breathe in the experiences that have brought us to who *I am right now*. It is time to Trust that the reason we are standing still is because it is exactly what is required at this very moment on the journey.

- *I have everything I need at this moment.*
- *I am in gratitude for all I have experienced.*
- *I am opening this door to allow many doors to be offered.*
- *I am here now.*
- *I give thanks and receive blessings.*
- *I have all the time in the world.*
- *I am the verse in Universe!*

Knowing When To Build

Standing still is an opportunity to allow us to become quiet, both in the active, external world and the internal activity of the inner world.

Knowing when to build is the process of consolidating. It is the time to dig in and evaluate where we are on our journey. It is the road reflected and evaluated—a time to quiet the world around us and ask our Self:

- *How am I doing so far?*
- *What lessons have I learned for my best and highest good?*
- *Am I okay?*
- *Is there joy in my daily life?*
- *Have I released the past?*
- *Have I taken good care of my body?*

· *What do I understand?*
· *Is this what I want to create today?*

Consolidation is the art of unification. It is the process of bringing everything together. In spiritual terms it is the time to take a good look at what works and what does not apply. It is a process of standing still and taking whatever time is necessary to decide what tools we have acquired and how best to move forward from the now. But if we do not understand what has brought us to this moment, if we are still having inner conflict about where we are today, then it is our greatest opportunity to take the Gift of standing still and reflect on what work we have done on our Self and what work we are still resisting.

The art of consolidating is separating the things that allow us to feel good about who and what we are and the things that are ready to be released. It is a spring cleaning for the Soul.

❖ **Take a look at what you have accomplished.**

· *I have released all past attachments to ex-boyfriends or ex-girlfriends.*
· *I am no longer a victim.*
· *I have changed careers.*
· *I am finding more Joy every day.*
· *I am taking care of my body temple.*
· *I am dating.*
· *I have cleaned out my closet.*
· *I am taking a cooking class.*
· *I am writing in my journal everyday.*
· *I am more loving to myself.*

❖ **Take a look at what does not allow you to feel good about your Self.**

My husband is abusive.
My weight is out of control.
I don't go out.
I have no hobbies.
I never travel to places I wish to go.
I hate my job.
I procrastinate too much.
I never have any time to myself.
It still isn't my turn.
I am still not doing charity work.
I do not meditate everyday.

❖ **Make a list of all the things you want to do this year.**

· *I'd like to walk every day.*
· *I am open to a better relationship with my family.*
· *I am going to love myself more.*
· *I want to go back to school and study a language.*
· *I am going to save ten percent of what I earn for me.*
· *I am setting intentions I can accomplish.*
· *I am allowing myself to express my Unique Self.*
· *I will take Tango lessons.*
· *I am going to be less critical of myself.*
· *I am adding Joy to my life.*
· *I am allowing myself to be more responsible to myself.*
· *I am meditating everyday.*

இ இ இ

The purpose for the art of consolidating is to unite all your accomplishments and plan what you desire to manifest from where you *already* are on your journey. *It is not the time to move forward* but to understand why you are standing still. It is not a time to build, but a time to plan what it is you wish to build. It is the time to take a stand by standing still, digging in and getting your life compact and united.

இ இ இ

Every planning stage is in knowing when to build.
Every planning stage is also in knowing what to build.

Being Too Insensitive To Participate in Divine Will

The art of consolidating is the process of uniting all the lessons and feeling good about them.

The art of planning is allowing our Self the freedom to express thoughts and be sensitive to how we feel about our plans.

The ability to participate with our Self in planning and the commitment to freedom is found through Faith that we are following our prayer.

Faith is the sincerity of intentions. Faith is the ability to add loyalty to our convictions and follow in the emotional stability of trust. Faith is the action of walking in the direction of our prayer, or desire. Being divinely guided is knowing that all thought is energy in action and in the nature of all things. Without faith, or the internal movement of right action we will struggle with the idea of "lack" in all things. It becomes a process of the human will to feel stuck and motionless, unsure there is support or connection to the Higher Conscious-Self.

The will center of the personal mind and human body process become further stuck because of lacking trust on the emotional plane. The Dangerous Mind is unwilling to listen to the deeper intuitive process of Higher Consciousness or God within. Confidence is relegated to out- sourcing for support because of the lack of self-esteem and clarity in the process of discovery through right action.

What occurs is a feeling of being acutely sensitive to what outside sources think about what we are building from the ground up. The process then becomes one of seeking outside approval in the form of advice.

Not believing we are able to make sound decisions in order to commit to the process, the advice and counsel of others become the voice of reason. Our personal agenda will determine who we turn to for opinion and counsel to further our plans. What happens often is the advice is based on the outsider's own personal agenda in the matter. When advice is asked an opinion is given whether good advice or to further another agenda.

It will then become an issue of whether or not we believe the opinion is for our best and highest good or merely the experience or agenda of another. It is amazing how often the advice of others holds more weight than the substance of our own deeper intuition within. Advice taken on good faith from friends, family and co-workers becomes the proof of what we endeavor and proof is not faith.

When we are more concerned with how *others think* about what we should do, or say, it is because we are too insensitive to our own feelings and willingness to participate in Divine Will, or right action.

The foundation for our building—the structure of our life— is being outsourced when our faith in another's actions is stronger than our belief in the inner guidance from the Higher Conscious-Self, or Universal Source.

Preoccupation in how others will feel and what they might think is giving our power away reducing confidence in our Self. Thinking we might step on toes or upset someone else becomes more important than whether we deserve to feel good about what we are planning and developing. Worrying about how anything we are planning may hurt someone else's feelings is the process of getting stuck in the commitment stage. Lacking the confidence to move forward without others' approval creates inner conflict. And if frustration arises from the lack of support from others, we may willfully decide to push ahead impatiently to accomplish what others and our Self affirm will not be successful. We will perhaps even make a commitment and sign a contract without reading the small print.

When we get in our own way and become stuck in the unwillingness to listen to our intuition and Higher Conscious Self we will give our trust away—outsource personal will—to the control of others. Instead of empowering our Self with trust in Divine Will, our plans become the property of everyone else's controlling interest and agendas.

It is better to take the time to consolidate all resources so we can better understand what we have to work with. Once this process has patiently been undertaken, it is then time to find gratitude and appreciation in what assets we have in our life. From this space it becomes easier to go through the process of planning, by applying faith, or action to empower us to look to our intuition for further trust of the Divine Light within, which will guide us into the application process to manifest our desires in Divine Order, or right action. If the plans we are wanting to commit to do not vibrate in a energy field of positive affirmed thought, then we need to ask our Self why we are making plans for anything not in our best and highest good?

If we are relying on others to support us, the Gift is showing us that we do not have faith and the confidence in our own action and ability to see the commitment all the way through to purpose. It is the beautiful reflection asking us to look inward to our own inner light—the small voice within—for the answers and to have the patience to allow the information to flow.

Self-doubt and the need to trust others before trusting our Self is one of the lower vibrations of the Dangerous Mind which develops from negative affirmed thought programs.

· *Other opinions including my own of myself are none of my business.*
· *I seek the answers I require from my Highest Self.*
· *I trust my life is in Divine Order and all is well within my world.*
· *Even though I cannot see it, touch it, taste it or smell it, I am always guided.*
· *I listen to my Inner Voice which blossoms during meditation.*
· *I look in the mirror and say, "I am the Divine Light within me."*

The Blame Game

When things go wrong who's to blame?

Most of the time we probably blame our Self! And then sometimes, when the frustration is too much it overflows sending the blame to someone or something else.

Blame is abusive. It is the Dangerous Mind's attempt to move the fault to anything or anybody but itself. The Dangerous Mind does not realize that all mistakes are simply changes in growth of conscious awareness, but thinks all mistakes are failures.

Whenever blame interferes with the process of developing a foundation through commitment, thinking clearly becomes unstable. The Dangerous Mind uses blame to attach to feelings connected to being unsupported and frustrated. Any frustration regarding plans manifests due to impatience and a belief of personal *entitlement* to have certain outcomes without having to do the work necessary to create the very same outcomes. Frustration is holding on to a belief that the world should write the check and simply hand it over. Frustration is then magnified to prevent any further attempts to move forward with all plans.

More importantly, *blame is judgment* and centered in *opinion.*

The blame game is how we view our Higher Self. When blaming our Self for being unable to commit to a firm decision, the Dangerous Mind will find fault with how the decision was made. It will look outside itself to find the fault, and the emotions attached to the fault will spark our unworthiness, unreliability in making sound choices and lack of self-trust. It is amazing how well the Dangerous Mind will attach such blame to both trust and worth since as a censure it has suggested we out-source the responsibility to other's opinions in the first place! The Dangerous Mind has already reflected our inability to make a sound decision on our own and was the very culprit who suggested we ask others what they think. Now it reminds us that there is no one to blame but our stupidity! Sneaky! The abusive nature of the blame game is to remind us constantly of all the scenarios we re-remember that are repeating once again. And if we cannot remember, then we should simply begin to beat our Self up for listening to anyone else.

· *Every time I help someone else I get screwed.*
· *The last time I tried this I got hurt.*
· *Why did I listen to you?*
· *It is entirely your fault!*
· *I never get a break!*
· *I knew you couldn't keep a secret!*
· *If you didn't spend so much, we wouldn't be in debt!*
· *I am so stupid!*
· *Why did I think I could pull it off?*
· *If I were smarter, I could pass.*

And on and on.

❖ **What do you blame yourself for?**
❖ **What do you hold others accountable for?**

Blame is directly connected to the beliefs we hold in our God box and the judgment manifests emotionally into the Dangerous Mind when we blame our Self. And whether we realize it or not, our Self is a reflection of our Higher Self and God within.

Blaming our Self is blaming God within.

· *God is punishing me.*
· *I must have been bad to be treated this way.*
· *God is never there when I need Him.*
· *I feel abandoned.*
· *I hate myself.*

The blame game is the lowest vibration we hold when thinking we are abandoned or betrayed. Our own false sense of ourselves, the mirror we hold up to our Self is saying, "I failed!" and we then blame inwardly. The Self-abuse is complete.

Both abuse and abandonment are created when the foundation of who I AM has been compromised at some point in our life. We wouldn't feel this way if we had developed a strong, emotional growth foundation and unfortunately we tend to then blame whoever raised us in the first place.

Now we might have spent a lifetime believing we will "never abandon or abuse anyone" the way we were and yet life often details the fact that this is not true. It is the reason for the blame. The emotionally sensitive Self, desiring for this statement to be true, is not in alignment with our beliefs and our Authentic Self knows this. The Authentic Self is offering us a Gift.

The Gift is that there is one person we abandon and betray all the time: our Self.

· *Every time we make the same mistakes over and over again.*
· *Every time we Trust someone more than our Self.*
· *Every time we give our power away.*
· *Every time we do not speak our Truth with Love.*
· *Every time we blame our Self.*
· *Every time you blame our God vibration, our Divine Light Within.*
· *Every time we beat our Self up.*

The blame game doesn't have a plan. It is going by the skin of our teeth. It is "believing" we will win the lottery. It is hope without a foundation. It is "trusting" everyone but our Higher Self. It is blind and reckless faith. It is Self-abuse. It is Self-abandonment. It is Self-betrayal.

No one wins the blame game.

The blame game is the alarm of Self-doubt, which prevents us from going inside our God box and re-examining our Beliefs. It is a Gift to beckon us to know the alarm is false and what we are required to do is go beyond the smoke and mirrors and examine what is preventing us from believing in our own ability to have a clear understanding of our Self. What is preventing us from trusting in a Higher Empowerment? Most importantly, why do we choose to abandon our Faith in our inner voice and betray our unique journey through Divine Will?

Self-empowerment begins when we realize we are able to have the outcome we desire of any plan undertaken, if we take each step systematically without missing or jumping impatiently to the next step.

· *I have everything I require to be whole.*
· *I am willing to be open to my Inner Voice and listen.*
· *I am on a unique journey of personal Love.*
· *All is well in my world.*
· *I follow Divine Will and cancel out any thoughts that are negative.*
· *I have all the time in the world.*

Standing on Solid Ground

There are many ways to plan a building, but the most important step is to make sure it is on solid ground. Even at the bottom of water, there is ground. It is the area used for a specific purpose and it is the solid base for a solid commitment. To be grounded is to stand firm on an area to create something from the ground up. It is the Earth we stand on and we call our present home. It is where all electrical charges return to a conducting point. It is where everything physical resides from a metaphysical expression. It is what we are made from on a physical plane of existence. It is the material of the stars.

When we begin to build anything it is from our ground zero and it is where the root that becomes the heart of the tree is created to explore potential and purpose.

Grounding is connecting our electrical energy force to our beautiful planet. We take it for granted and we journey upon it for a lifetime without ever considering how much it comforts us; how willing it is to hold a singular intention.

When we are spending too much time in our mind with all the lofty thoughts and ideas whirling around, it is important to remember to stand up and jump up and down and know we are still on the ground.

Today is the best day to know we are a part of this great adventure. This planetary ship spins through space like a great cruiser on a maiden voyage through the landscape called space. It has everything necessary to accommodate us: great food, cabins, spas and recreational facilities. It is quiet as a mouse as it moves along thousands of miles per hour without need of repairs. It has scenic views and panoramic vistas to soothe our eyes and accommodates our every need without asking for anything in return. It is as solid as a rock and shares mystical, wondrous rainbow skies. It has the perfect environmental temperatures to suit everyone's requirements.

Why are we here?

We are here to enjoy all the pleasures offered and to relax, but we are also here to discover and explore our fullest potential. Nothing more, nothing less.

Enjoy it.

Walk, run, play, dance, sing, paint, and build dreams on something worthwhile and of value to everyone.

When we remember to ground, our plans will take roots, grow and blossom into the world we are making up!

Consider the lilies of the field—they do nothing. They toil not, spin not and struggle not. Yet, they grow and are clothed by the universal mind of God.

❖ **What can you do today and every day to ground?**

· *I will dance.*
· *I will play.*
· *I will walk in the evening at sunset.*
· *I will learn Tai Chi.*
· *I will paint a mural.*
· *I will sit under a tree and plan.*
· *I will plant a garden.*
· *I will build a shed.*
· *I will climb a mountain.*
· *I will sing to the stars.*
· *I will love the Earth.*
· *I will run a marathon.*
· *I will give back to the planet.*
· *I will make an offering to the river.*
· *I will go to the beach.*
· *I will kiss a tree.*
· *I will create a bouquet.*
· *I will go on a picnic.*
· *I will plant a tree.*

- *I will talk to the Spirit of the Earth.*
- *I will rest upon it.*
- *I will play with animals.*
- *I will protect it.*
- *I will embrace it.*
- *I will adventure upon it.*
- *I will hike on it.*
- *I will climb a tree.*
- *I will write a poem.*
- *I will call her Mother.*
- *I will sit on it.*
- *I will swim in it.*
- *I will cruise upon it.*
- *I will row a boat.*
- *I will dance in the rain.*
- *I will water it when it is thirsty.*
- *I will clean the skies.*
- *I will know I am safe.*
- *I will breathe.*
- *I will enjoy the cruise.*

And most importantly,
I will appreciate how beautiful the world has been to me.

A fear of success is expressed in instability. Being stable is a *deliberate intention connected to commitment.* Being committed is reflected in relationships, homes and work. When any one of these aspects become about commitment, stability will be in motion. If, there is instability, inner conflicts will upset the balance. The lack of balance will cause inner stability to be under scrutiny emotionally, physically, mentally and spiritually. Every commitment is mirrored in how well the foundations are built in family, education and physical activity. If at any level the underlying feelings are not in alignment with the outcome, then the foundation will appear suspect. When we feel we are unable to succeed in our desires, the best place to look is inside our Self.

Discovery

1. Take a look at your relationships. Are they positively affirmed or not? Remembering that like attracts like, examine what aspects you do not like about others and then look in the mirror.

2. Take a look at your job. Are you doing what you love?

3. Take a look at your education. Are you continually growing and developing new positive affirmed thoughts?

4. Take a look at your physical activities. Are you walking, meditating, dancing, and singing?

5. What commitments are you afraid to make? And why?

6. Take a look at what you have accomplished. Write them down and examine how your accomplishments help to create the person you are today. Then appreciate and value all that you have created.

7. Make a list of what does not allow you to feel good about your Self. A relationship, a vocation, and/or life? Can you let go of this list?

8. Make a list of all the things you want to do this year. Did you place them on a vision board?

9. What do you blame yourself for? Others? Why? Now can you let it all go?

10. What can you do today and every day to ground?

Everyday Affirmations

No one's opinion of me is any of my business.

My opinion of myself is none of my business.

I seek the answers I require from my Highest Self.

I trust my life is in Divine Order.

Even though I cannot see it, touch it, taste it or smell it, I am guided.

I listen to my Inner Voice.

I am the Divine Light within me.

I have everything I need at this moment.

I am in gratitude for all I have experienced.

I am opening this door to allow many doors to be offered.

I am here now.

I give thanks and receive blessings.

I am the verse in Universe!

You must begin to trust yourself. If you do not, then you will forever be looking to others to prove your own merit to you, and you will never be satisfied. You will always be asking others what to do and at the same time resenting those from whom you seek such aid.

- Author unknown

Chapter 5

Aspects of Love

Love as an Experience

In all that has been recorded in history regarding love, very little has been written about what love is in itself. There is only the language of love. It is understood as the dialogue of love. It is the words we write and say, it is the feelings we express to one another and to ourselves in so many ways. But when asked, "What is love?" often we can only speak of it through our own experiences.

There is the love between mother and infant. It is a bond manifesting at the beginning of the experience of birth and it may be nurtured for a lifetime. It is considered to be the most sacred of all experiences that are known and the fiber that creates the cohesion of progress and evolution. It is the strong affection for another arising out of kinship or personal ties. It is the experience of maternal feelings for a child.

But it is not necessarily true that it occurs every time. Many children are abandoned or aborted early on. It is not necessary to love a child for growth. The child can be raised and cared for without love, yet still discover the experience of love in many ways throughout his or her lifetime. So what is this thing called love and where does it come from? How has love evolved in human beings and why? And why is it so difficult to say what love is?

The sexual experience has been attached romantically to love, but this is only a recent development, since the 19th century. Since then, it has been present in poetry, literature and the movies. It is not just sexual but something more. It is something one may do in an environment of "making love." Yet the sexual experience in itself is not love. It is only the desire and the instinct to satisfy an urge. Without love the world would still have sex. There would still be procreation.

But throughout time there has been the connection with sex and love. Love's inseparability from sexuality has been taken for granted by writers historically. *Amour* is love connected to passion attached to someone desired. But is it love?

Insofar as that love has been healthy in expanding beyond loving one Self into the love of others, and strengthening family relationships and expanding the unity of nations, it is of great benefit and is represented in history.

Without love there might have been mayhem and chaos and the human species might not evolve. Love is important in maintaining order and compassion to fellow human beings. It is what we acknowledge as important and justified; yet we still cannot define love without attaching it to something or somebody.

Beyond the mother and child union and the sexual interpretation of love there is the concept of mystical love. It is often attached to religions in the form of the love of God or the belief in a loving family and neighbors. Attaching love to a social group for acceptance or to a larger unseen force is to place love outside the center of the Self as an extension of love. The importance of projecting the experience of love beyond the love of Self is promoted by religions, both traditional and non-traditional, throughout the world. But is there such a thing as religious love? Is it possible to transfer love to something that is not a human experience? What then is the model for God?

Love has been defined as an attraction, common interest and as affection. It is the term of endearment of something benevolent and unselfish. It is also explained as an object of devotion, admiration, enthusiasm and adoration. Whenever love is spoken of, it is always connected to an action or a projection, as the experience of love.

The experience of love is the vibration of the Self in evolution. It is a human process through experience moving deeper into the realm of the Soul. It is the Self in search of the Soul.

The art of love is in understanding the meaning of love.

The aspects of love are present in the attachments we have with our children, family, lovers and community. We develop the deeper meaning of our Self through these attractions. They are real and they feel real. All these aspects reflect vibrations back to our Self to connect us with our Soul.

The Soul is the home of the Higher Self and Higher Consciousness and God.

Religions throughout the world have spread the message of love. They talk of the great mysteries and the laws of love. The requirements are to have compassion, place others before your Self, and to love God or gods. The mysteries are mysterious and continue to be abstract. And God is something outside of the human understanding, something bigger than the human experience. God is then included in the concept of something mysterious that cannot be defined any better than love. How then can we be empathetic to concepts?

Is God love?

Connecting to the empathy of love is in all understanding gathered vicariously through the experiences of feelings and thoughts of another without having any feelings or thoughts fully communicated in an objectively explicit manner. It becomes a matter of being empathetic and projecting feelings into an object so that it can be infused with the feeling of love.

When we experience the emotional feeling of love or the object of our internal feelings of love. The object is there to reflect how we feel when we perceive it. In other words, when "I love you" is spoken, it is only a reflection of the feelings inside the perceiver.

When we say, "I love you" as a communication of feelings we are really saying, "Because of you, I can feel love inside myself." And the feeling inside our Self is creating a higher vibration in our Self, tapping into the center, the place we call the heart. It is not the physical heart but the Heart-Self at the center of Universal Mind, or core. And the core of Being is the Soul-Self in our higher consciousness. By connecting to anything or anyone that feels good the center of our emotional-Self is centered and feels love. This is then expressed as, "I Love you." The words are the outward communication of the vibration of love intensified in our Soul-Self.

"I Love You" is the Self communicating with the Divine Light Within.

The art of love is the empathic process of connecting the basic-conscious-emotional-sensitive Self to the Divine Light Heart-Self within. Without love we would be unable to vibrate higher to have the total experience of God.

Love is the heightened perception and attention on the journey of knowing.

The Journey

There is an infinite map of our Life. In the physical realm it has a beginning and an ending. We often do not believe we have anything to say about either place. We have come into this world through an expression of another's aspect of love and we exit at some time without having any say. Whether we believe that we chose our parents or not, the physical aspect of the Self is veiled from really knowing if this is true. And, even if we have decided when we are departing from this planet, it normally has simply been left as a surprise. Even though there have been many ideas written about the afterlife, most people will say they are not sure what is on the other side of this life. The opportunity to sneak over and play for a time and then come back is not easy. So what is known of this life, before or after, is behind a veil of mystery. We only know for sure that we are on a journey.

At times the journey appears to be planned out and at other times it seems to be spontaneous. It can feel guided and sometimes it can be blind instinct, but it is always forward moving and the journey is a process of maturing and growing. We know we are going somewhere, but where?

The one known factor is: We know where we have been. Only here can we reflect and see patterns on the road leading to this very moment. All we have to do is look back and start from where we remember and move forward until today. It is always there to be reflected upon, if we take the time to follow the path.

At times the journey has been smooth and at other times, tumultuous. It has been broad and narrow filled with loss and gain and pauses along the way. But one thing is for sure: It has been the journey of a lifetime!

The journey is an opportunity for progress.

Journey is defined as traveling from one place to another. It is never the same place. Sometimes the road looks familiar but it is never the same road on the same day. The journey is in constant change. It is the keystone, the association that is depended upon for support. The journey is our support.

There are many ways to take the journey and far too many emotions regarding the attachment to our travels. We can love it, hate it, find joy in it, be fearful of it, or simply be bored by it, but there is always some emotional attachment to it. Whatever attachment we place on life at any given moment will support the outcome. How we feel about the journey will be the guidance system moving us from place to place. It can be supported by love or by fear, but either way there is infinite support.

The choice is in how we feel about it today. Whatever feelings have been *already* associated with an intention will determine how well the creative process will unfold. Once the commitment is made, it becomes the next opportunity to center on the intention and trust in the process. Trusting in the process will center the emotional guidance system to carry the intention to fruition of purpose. It is the most important aspect in manifesting the highest outcome.

When the emotional guidance system is centered and balanced—including being grounded—the vibration magnifies as an aspect of love.

Love is Good in the making.

Love is the noble impulse that moves the lofty dream into a lofty manifestation. It allows us to decide whether we love as an attachment—conditionally or unconditionally—or love transparently.

Transparent love is love that needs no reflection.

Love is the Journey.

The journey is courageous. With every step we take we are awakening the I Am. Whether life is through conflict (contest, competition, emulation, rivalry, strife, striving, tug-of-war, warfare or discord) or freedom (exemption, immunity, prerogative, privilege, or right) it is a necessity. Life is the journey we are destined to travel.

Love is the journey to awaken the I Am.

When we skip the step of moving any intention without being centered in the Heart— the emotional guidance system—a cautionary and insecure journey will be created. Yet so many people do not trust love to guide them. Not trusting love is the same as being unwilling to trust the God within. It only depends on personal will instead of Divine Will, because an untrusting nature is not sure what Divine Will means. It becomes only a life journeyed by literalism (observable fact) where everything seen has more value than what is unseen. The blind and reckless journey is not a sojourn allowing leaps of faith through commitment, rather it is a journey created irresponsibly. It is made often in societies where it is better to fear God than embrace love.

Love walks above the radar.

Life is a journey of necessities. It is necessary to eat and breathe. It is a necessity to procreate and feed the young. It is a necessity to build shelters and farms. It is a necessity to stay warm. But love is not a necessity. Love is the navigator we can choose to guide us on our journey. Why do so many choose to do it alone?

Love is the attraction to love.

The human journey is an aspect of love. It is the road that teaches, bestows, endows, and Gifts along the way.

When love is least expected, wanted or ignored, it is still offered.

Love abides within the very fabric of the journey. It is the parchment on which the journey is inscribed. Even as the fabric of love is traveled unseen, it resonates and vibrates as a knowing.

It is written in mystical text, I am to love my neighbor as I already love myself. Who will speak words of love to me, if I do not speak them first to myself?

Trust

Trust resides in the Beautiful Mind and self-doubt is in the abode of the Dangerous Mind. The duality of the mind is an illusion. Both aspects are the polarity to create a balance. They are both real yet only in the Conscious-Self. It is a higher vibration to play in the Beautiful Mind than to work in the Dangerous Mind. But even the Beautiful Mind places opinions, or judgments within the perceptions of thought as identity. However the opinions, or point of view of the Beautiful Mind will vibrate to the positive state of feelings (courage, willingness, peace and love). The Dangerous Mind which will vibrate more to the negative state of feelings (pride, anger, apathy and fear).

Judgment is an opinion.

Trust is a difficult concept for many people. We will tell ourselves that it is very difficult to trust in anyone including our own Self. They do not know why, but it is how they feel. So how can we trust love? Especially when all the attachments we have had to love have abandoned, hurt or betrayed us? We sometimes believe that trust is *earned* and love is costly. We hold these beliefs because of past negative affirmed experiences with the perception of trust.

· *I trusted them and they let me down.*
· *It is hard to find someone trustworthy.*
· *I trusted them and they broke my heart.*
· *I trusted them and they stole money from me.*
· *I trusted God and He let me down.*
· *I don't know how to trust in anything.*

Sometimes trust is defined by a destiny-driven paradigm. It is dependent or contingent on a future outcome. Trust, like love, becomes attached to something or someone as a reliance of future payment or assurance. And when the outcome does not live up to the expectation then trust becomes the issue, not the something or someone. Trust becomes the suspect and what may have been an agenda of the Beautiful Mind now falls prey to the doubt in the Dangerous Mind. Trust becomes judged.

Once an opinion becomes a belief held in the God box then it becomes a truth and it is no longer thought of as an opinion. It becomes harder and harder to rely on trusting anything. No wonder it is difficult for some people to trust in the "now" when trust is connected to hope and credit, which are both destiny-driven outcomes!

Trust arises from grounding. It is not hope but faith. It is assurance that whatever the outcome, it was made through good constructive planning and commitment. If an intention is created from feeling unsure, through lack of clarity—developed through negotiation—and sound commitment it will not evolve into trust. Trust will be bypassed in the necessary step-by-step procedure, outlined in the first four chapters of this book, and fall prey to unclear application. If trust cannot be arrived at, it is because all the steps leading to it have not been taken on the journey. When we do not trust in what we feel then it will be impossible to love it. For love and trust reside in the center of our magnetic vibrations and touch all aspects of the emotional stability of the heart.

Trust is love assured.

Trust is holding the assurance of love. It cannot be broken—only misunderstood by beliefs attached to the emotional, imbalanced Self in conflict with the duality of the mind. To understand trust is to go beyond the Conscious Self and commit to love. Trust is an aspect of love in harmony with the Universal Mind not in the duality of the Beautiful/Dangerous Mind.

❖ **How often do you trust others' opinions more than your own?**
❖ **How easy is it to give away your trust?**

Others also give trust away easily. It is sent to us in the mail, or delivered C.O.D. It is written in the form of a check or plastic credit cards. Trust is the assurance that you will pay your bills after using a service. Trust is given every day, and every day it is broken. Trust has become a word connected to obligation, not love. So every time the bills are overdue, the checks bounce, or the creditors are calling, the word trust becomes weakened and mistrusted. Trust becomes unreliable and is no longer perceived as love. It takes on a persona of its own and blossoms into any feelings and negative affirmed thoughts connected to the word trust. The vibration of trust is reduced and holds fault and blame.

Trust, like love, becomes attached to something or someone instead of being an aspect of the heart. Trust becomes uneasy and un-assured connecting to any past feelings of re-remembered betrayals or abandonment. *Why should I trust you or trust anything?* Trust can also become attached to the five senses. Many people will only trust what they can smell, see, touch, taste or physically feel. Trust, like love is no longer the Knower residing within, but is the lessons from experiences without.

❖ **How many times have you relegated trust to others?**
❖ **Do you easily trust others before trusting your Self?**
❖ **How do you define trust?**
❖ **Does trust have faith in the "now" or give you hope in the future?**
❖ **When is trust a lower vibration? Reflect on past experiences.**
❖ **When is love attached to negative affirmed thoughts?**
❖ **Is there a limit to your trust?**
❖ **Do you limit the amount of love you give to others?**
❖ **When did another naively exploit you?**
❖ **How much does your expectation influence your experience?**

Trust is assurance; it is not destiny-driven. It *relies* on intuition and "gut feelings." Trust may be attached to teachings, experiences and negative/positive affirmed thoughts in the mind or a self-aware inner voice magnetizing love. The personal mind believes it must protect itself and will validate or reject everything from its opinions concluded from past exploitations reinforced by facts (re-remembered thoughts replayed over and over again). The heart is grounded in knowing that the personal mind is only a small aspect of a great Universal Mind that encompasses All-Knowing. The All-Knowing Universal Mind, or God is where every thing begins and ultimately returns. To trust is to begin to understand in this wisdom. It is beyond the five senses and is meta-consciousness. Knowing is beyond, behind, below and above the personal mind and any identity we hold in our thoughts.

Knowing is an aspect of love.

As we begin to confidently trust ourselves and listen to our gut feelings, or intuition—which is an integral part of a spiritual journey we are all ultimately experiencing—we create the changes necessary for growth in consciousness. Allowing trust to be connected to our intuition and the deeper wisdom leads to understanding that trust is the spiritual center of love and dwells in the heart of the Higher Mind or God within. With intuition resting in our left hand, wisdom in our right hand and trusting love in our centered Self we become an emotionally balanced guidance system. The need to feel safe in the personal mind will subside into knowing we are safe, self-assured, complete and fulfilled in the Authentic Self.

Trust is committed to love.

Am I Free?

Another aspect of love is freedom. The art of freedom is the absence of necessity, coercion, or constraint in choice or action. Freedom is a quality or a state of Being. Freedom resonates in love allowing for the highest vibrations of the emotionally balanced Self to become the Authentic Self. Freedom dismantles the illusions of duality in life and transcends the limitations of a fragmented body-mind-spirit.

Because of the diversity of experiences we interpret freedom in many different ways. Sometimes it is the freedom to be over-indulgent, self-indulgent or to take advantage of others or nature. Oftentimes it is viewed as the freedom to do anything and every-thing in the breadth of experiences rather than the *depth* of a singular experience. The personal mind will interpret freedom as what is lacking in our lives. It is the measurement that mirrors the restrictions and confinements in life. The lack of freedom in jobs, relationships, sexuality, nations, and religions reflects how little freedom we have in the first place and freedom becomes an ideal instead of a reality. Freedom is a concept that needs restriction and confinement because too much of it will lead to moving outside the boundaries set by church and state as society. Freedom is something talked about like an extra-marital affair; a fantasy not to be embodied. Freedom has a broad range of applications from total absence of restraint to merely a sense of not being unduly hampered or frustrated.

Freedom is liberation.

Janis Joplin sang "Freedom is another word for nothing left to lose." It is what we have after everything else has been stripped away. This may be closer to the truth than we think, but stripped away from what? Freedom is being stripped of the ties that bind us in most cases. Freedom from debt, burdens, responsibilities, relationships, children, obligations, compulsions, addictions, or a myriad of other things! Freedom is even perceived to be the ability to have everything we want.

❖ **What is freedom to you?**

Freedom is only as free as what is determined by societal boundaries with respect to everyone else living in it. Freedom is limited by the personal mind and therefore not free. Yet within these restraints lies the opportunity for freedom. In many cases we can be free to make the choices we decide regarding our bodies—whether to take care of the body temple favorably or not. Obviously many millions of people are not able to have such freedom because of starvation from national strife.

The personal mind is limited by how conscious and aware it is of its own limitations, and by how much allowance of the creative flow of thoughts is unrestricted by fear.

So where does freedom reside?

Freedom is the Universal Mind.
We are but the individual thoughts in the Universal Mind of God.

It is the place where nothing is lost and everything is infinite possibility. It is the answer to the *"Who Am I?"* that the multifaceted fragmented Self asks over and over again. It is the longing of the desire to know we are One through Self-realization.

The journey of the Soul, being human, is to discover freedom is already ours. All we need to do is stand up and be free. For those of us who suffer along the way, the journey to inner freedom is all that is truly desired. For those of us who believe the journey of the world is an adventure it will be easy to understand. But whether the journey is long-suffered or a joyful, fun-filled adventure, the Soul is waiting for us to arrive at knowing that all roads are Self liberated!

· *I am free to change my beliefs.*
· *I am free to open my heart.*
· *I am free to express myself, fully.*
· *I am free to be authentic.*
· *I am free to know love.*
· *I am free to accept trust.*
· *I am free in my Soul.*
· *I am free from the duality of my personal mind.*
· *I am free in my opportunity for progress.*
· *I am free to experience.*
· *I am free to know myself.*
· *I am free to say, "Yes" to life!*
· *I am free to experience transparent love.*

Self-Love—The Gift

Self-Love is accepting and allowing people to Be who they are on their journey of Self-awareness. It starts with allowing the Self to be who "I Am." Self-love is surrendered to the Higher Self, Higher Consciousness, Universal Mind, or God within. It is acknowledging that we are courageous, willing, charitable, appreciative, gracious, peaceful and joyful saying, "Yes to life!" and also saying, "I am trust-worthy!" It is ultimately surrendering to the God box of all beliefs even when we do not know what is truth. It is surrendering to our deepest feelings that speak of wonderment and adventure. Self-love is understanding that hope is illusory existing without faith (action) and trust (assurance) which are two of the nine important ingredients on our journey of holding a vision of Authentic Self. Dismantling the beliefs that do not allow us to accept people for who they are is a God box exploiting our power, judging the world, and holding negatively affirmed thoughts as opinion of everyone. When we think negative affirmed thoughts of others we are only going against a manifestation of our own Self. When we are jealous, envious, distrusting, belittling, impatient, angry or hateful towards any part of life, life will have no choice but to be the same to us.

· *I love to hate.*
· *I love war.*
· *I love to be prejudiced.*
· *I love to control.*
· *I love to bully.*
· *I love to fight.*
· *I love to gossip.*
· *I love to beat myself up.*
· *I love being the victim, or "poor me!"*
· *I love being the martyr.*
· *I love to win.*
· *I love to hide.*
· *I love to hate myself.*
· *I love to run away.*
· *I love being the hero.*
· *I love to be needed.*

❖ **What do you love to feel that is not Self-Love?**

Self-Love is the evolutionary experience for elevated consciousness: Self-Love is the Gift.

It is knowing we can love the Self without understanding why the journey so far has been difficult or painful. It is the Gift we can give to the Self that no one else is able to give us. It is ours and ours *transparently* to receive. It is the Gift as soon as we realize there is nothing to wait for, want for, or need any longer. We can make-believe we are loved or love others but without loving the Self within, there is no love to know.

Self-love is the awareness we value the Self. It is allowing the Soul to whisper in our ear what we cannot remember because of a life filled with abuse, hunger, pain, suffering, addiction, loneliness and believing we are misunderstood. It is realizing the value of how much we have given to others to empower them even when unable to empower ourselves. It is taking the time to look back over the journey we have made so far and access the depth of it. So far, the journey no longer needs to be viewed from the path, but can now be seen in wholeness by rising above it and looking down over the whole map to see our landmarks. It is taking the time everyday to evaluate *generously* all we have contributed to others and to our own Self. Self-love is the conscious positive affirmed thoughts repeating, "I am that!" in everything.

Self-love is present in all the different aspects of love we have *already* experienced in past, present and future. It is letting go—forgiving—of all criticism and blame to the Self in all of us. Self-love is able to forgive the Self in everyone because wherever a person is in his or her present state of consciousness is the "life I could be living." It is the Gift that allows us to appreciate all life and to have a charitable heart and thoughtful mind. Self-love offers the Gift of joy as the Highest Good within each of us.

Self-love surrenders to our Highest Vibration of Soul Love.

Self-love is the journey on the river to Self-awareness. When we are aware, so are the trees and the stars!

The journey from Being human to Consciously waking up to Self-love to Mindful awareness is the river flowing into Self-actualization of the Authentic Self.

The Gift is for us. It begins and ends and begins again beyond time and space. It is not taught or learned. It is only aware of its Self.

Everything we have experienced has led us to this moment: the journey into the personal transformation of Self-love.

Transparent Love

Of all the aspects of love, the most deeply meaningful is transparent love. It is diaphanous and clear. It is Universal Mind-Spirit-Soul Love! It is the I Am of the Heart, the center of the mind of God! Soul love is beyond the basic, conscious and emotional Self. It resides in the space where all Love is allowed beyond the personal mind.

Soul Love is transparent, diaphanous and clear.

Soul Love in the higher vibration echoes and whispers, "Remember me."

It is the current that flows through the heart and floats to the conscious Mind, waxing and waning in perfect harmony. It is the small little voice that softly speaks, "I am free," even when we do not believe it to be true.

The Soul in Divine Love is absolute freedom. Divine Love

whispers softly the Highest Vibration to the Soul saying, "I Am!"

Transparent love is without condition, judgment or blame. It is the road we are traveling with every breath we take without truly understanding it in the personal mind. The Soul is where the journey from the unmanifest, universal Beingness flows through thought, expression, consciousness and spiritual heart before arriving in awareness as purpose. It is the river of Life on the journey to remembering WHO I AM.

In our minds we are in the dual state of the Beautiful and Dangerous Mind waxing and waning between what we believe and what we know—good and bad, right and wrong, up and down, yes and no, loss and gain, and life and death. Even with love we partition it between conditional and unconditional aspects. Yet when we accept that all is understood in the infinite singularity of the One expressed in the infinite possibility of All, then we no longer rely on old paradigms of unaware choices.

We begin to realize whether we think the true Will of the God-Self is divided between the human and Divine, the realization that the perceived division in reality is—there is no difference how the journey goes. Both "choices" are one in the same! In the Divine Will everything is perfect just the way it is, and all actions or inactions are part of a greater plan that is expressing itself exactly how it should be and all is well and perfect. In the human will the personal mind thinks and believes there are many choices to make and depending on the choices made the outcome will be easier or harder through the lessons learned, the mistakes made, and the roads traveled in between. At any given point we can look back at all the hardships, the pain and suffering, the losses and gains, and even the betrayals and denials and realize that everything we have created, experienced and discovered has led us to where we are right now. And without those moments we would not be who we are today. So we ask ourselves

Perfect Will

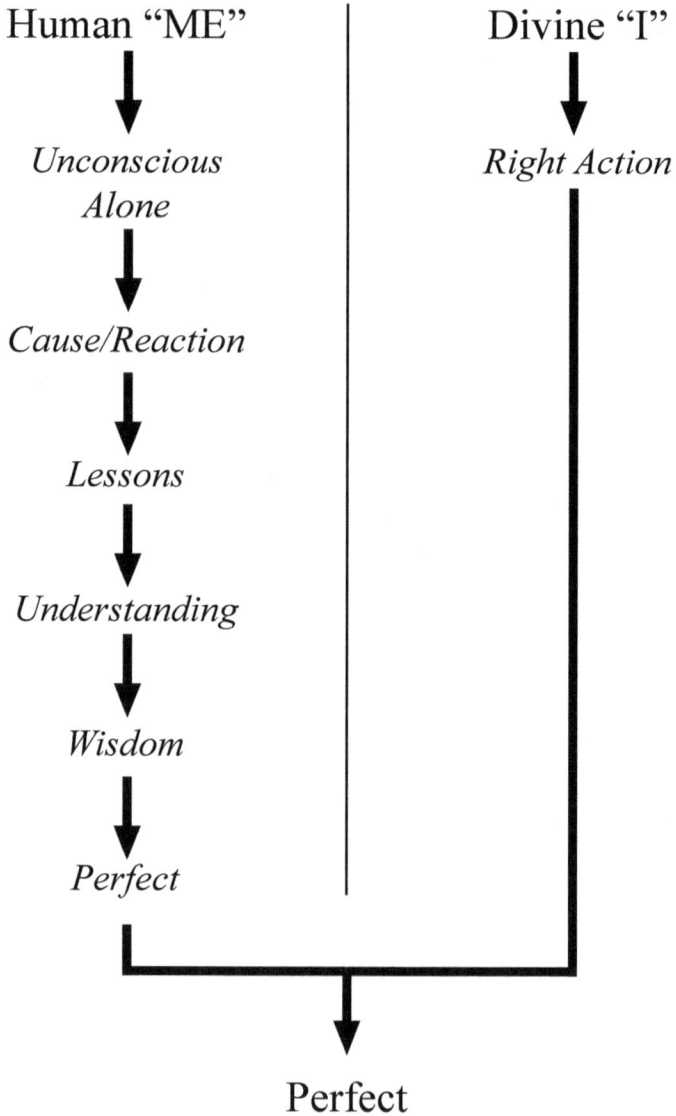

Human "ME"   Divine "I"

Unconscious   *Right Action*
Alone

Cause/Reaction

Lessons

Understanding

Wisdom

Perfect

Perfect

if we could take it all back and start fresh are we willing to give up what we now know about who we are and start over? Most people will say no.

So near the end of our journeys here on Earth there is perhaps the realization that we would not be where we are if we had not lived and made the choices we made. That life on Earth plays out exactly the way it does and that is exactly how it is supposed to be. All is well and perfect anyway we chose.

In the Divine Will everything is as it is meant to be and perfect in right action (a succession of success) and alignment with the Universal Mind. In the human will everything is the illusion of choice and is as it should be and perfect. Perfect is perfect indeed and the illusion of duality is simply an illusion.

At-One-Ment

At-one-ment is the exemplifying of human oneness with Love. It is the process of tearing down the wall of separation between all aspects of Love and knowing there is only love. The journey so far has been a map to the Soul of each Self. There is no separation, no multi-faceted Self, only our Highest Potential expressing itself in multi-faceted aspects of the Self. There is so much said on the subject of Oneness, Self-Actualization, Awareness, the God Within, the Higher Self and the human reflection. It sounds wonderful but seemingly beyond reach. It is something that only the few who are wise, sincere and charitable can attain. It is explained over and over again as the great mystery that is some sort of puzzle to figure out and put together. It is the "catch-22" that says, "To have it, you must know it first."

There is only one mystery, and it is when we look in the mirror and wonder what we are looking at instead of seeing the beautiful human expression as perfect and whole. What we are is the keystone that grounds all Being into reality. We are the sap, the goo of creation manifested into an expression that experiences everything without boundaries. We are star material on a starship cruiser manifesting our potential on a journey of infinite possibility. We are what God is made of.

We are love in the making.

It is said that the only constant is change (the Eternal Now and Presence). But the Soul knows, the only thing that is infinitely constant is Absolute Love which is *Infinite* Intelligence or God.

Discovery

1. How often do you trust others' opinions more than your own?

2. How easy is it to give away your trust?

3. How many times have you relegated trust to others?

4. Do you easily trust others before your Self?

5. How do you define Trust?

6. Does trust have faith in the "now" or give you "hope" in the future?

7. When is trust a lower vibration?

8. When is Love a lower vibration?

9. Is there a limit to your trust?

10. Do you limit love?

11. When did another naively exploit you?

12. How much does your expectation influence your experience?

13. What is freedom to you?

14. What do you love to feel that is not Self-Love?

Everyday Affirmations

I am free to change my beliefs.

I am free to open my heart.

I am free to express myself, fully.

I am free to be Authentic.

I am free to Love.

I am free to Trust.

I am free in my Soul.

I am free from the duality of my Mind.

I am free in my opportunity for progress.

I am free to experience.

I am free to Know.

I am free to say, "YES" to Life!

I am free to express transparent Love.

I am Love in the manifesting.

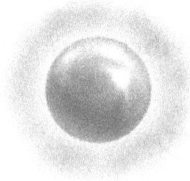

Love yourself first and everything else falls into line. You really have to love yourself to get anything done in this world.

- Lucille Ball

Chapter 6

The Divine Relationship

A Flexible Will

Entwined in the story of evolutionary human consciousness is the struggle of the two aspects of the Will. We are joined and in conflict with the higher understanding of the Divine Will and the Free Will of our humanity. Divine Will is often believed to be the holy ground of the Higher Self, intervening on behalf of a higher power when humanity needs assistance and guidance. Free Will is placed in the story of humanity as the guardian of our Spirit to be creative through personal choice and determination. One is an aspect of a higher realm and the other, placed in the domicile of Man, is sometimes in conflict and struggle and then at other times in harmony and partnership. The illusion of the personal mind thinks the human will has choice because it perceives from thought that there is separateness from Divine Will. The personal mind does not comprehend that all is in right action in life but instead, holds opinion and judgment to be more valuable for survival in life.

The unconscious mind perceives God and Man as separate and creates cause and effect, which create lessons to evolve from. Cause and effect remains an infinite loop in the unconscious mind by only reacting on itself and manifesting another effect to react upon. There is no choice in unconscious mind only reaction. Choice exists within conscious awareness of right action, or Divine Will.

What is Divine Will if not choice? How do we know which one we are following within the human experience?

Like most relationships there is struggle and conflict due to lack of communication and understanding. It is the same with all aspects of Will. The Divine Will holds the intention of the perfection of love and we hold many intentions, many not for our best and highest good.

Within the aspects of the human psyche a double triune exists. We are of Body, Soul and Spirit. This is the trinity of being human on Earth. In the energy field there is also the trinity of Physical (material), Etheric (heavens) and Astral (visionary). The Union is the perfection of all parts and at the center of the connection is the Soul having complimentary feminine/masculine energies. We are of Heaven and Earth. We are what the stars are made of and we are Divine.

Human Beings are being humans in partnership with the Divine Universe.

In fact, when we take a closer look at the word human, we see that it is composed of two words. Hu translated as God. *Man* is the spiritual image and likeness of God—the full representation of Mind. Thus, *human* means God-Mind.

The Divine Will is the perfection of Justice (right action) and Mercy (a blessing that is an act of divine favor or compassion), and the Human Will is the perfection of Choice. They comprise the flexible relationship of the Soul as liquid Truth.

The only conflict is in the duality of the Self. The relationship is with the choice to listen to the Higher Self and flow in the harmony of life or to *believe* the only Will we have is the Will to survive and strive for attainment and completion.

❖ **What are you striving to attain?**

The Divine Will is Who I Am in the Higher Self in *partnership* with Who I Am in the Trinity of the Hu-man as Body, Soul and Spirit-Self. It is Creator Being creative!

Only the human-Self judges the creation holding an *opinion* of creation. The human-Self judges against personal identity standards and holds the intention of comparison. The human-Self manifests the intention of the *ideal*, the standard of perfection, beauty or excellence. This opinion or judgment is the self-improvement program of the human being and the standard is how we judge against all higher standards. Ideals are often the standard that prevents human beings from escaping the burden of perfectionism. Ideals become the highest standards in the God box preventing the opportunity for true accomplishment, often ending in a conclusion of feeling unable to fully realize the desire for true happiness, so the attempt becomes futile. Why try to attain something that is unattainable? Perfectionism is a goal that begins as an ideal.

Perfectionism always loses.

Perfectionism is often attached to the Divine Will. It is something to strive to connect with, but often it is seen as something that cannot be attained. The Divine Will is attached to the human concept of an ideal; however, it is not an ideal but the Human evolution *in* perfection.

❖ **What do you believe Divine Will to be?**

When perfectionism is attached to the Dangerous Mind it becomes the measure for comparison. No matter how good something is, it can always be better.

· *I lost ten pounds but I still do not look as good as I want.*
· *I love the piano but I can never play as well as Mozart.*
· *I look great but I am still not beautiful.*
· *I am not sure because I can never make the best choice.*
· *I am smart but I am not always sure I am smart enough.*
· *It was a great party but it would have been better if only I had hired a bartender.*

Perfectionism is the trap of never being good enough. It is the hall monitor wearing the badge of self-doubt. It is the gatekeeper of the Dangerous Mind preventing us from tapping into the Divine Will. The gatekeeper is here to stop us from applying our intention for the best and highest good, always telling us to turn back and doubt inner trust in the plan. The Dangerous Mind will protect itself by implementing *censors.*

· *Are you sure you will succeed?*
· *Did you miss a step?*
· *What is there to understand?*
· *You have made it this far but now it will only get harder.*
· *There is always room for self-improvement.*

The human will has an attachment to opinions and improvements. The Divine Will is progress, *creation unfolding* through continual growth of consciousness into awareness.

Progress is the expedition, the journey through excellence, and excellence takes time and practice. Progress is without judgment and is a sojourn of joy in application of the vision towards excellence and success. Progress is flexible Divine Will in partnership with the human will, collaborating in the blended brilliant creativity of the Spirit of the God Mind, manifesting into the Soul, utilizing the Self being Human.

The Practical Visionary

At the Center of the Conscious Self is the Creative Mind of Higher Consciousness or God, the collaboration between the abundant flow of thought applied to individual purpose. The Conscious Self is the Creator bringing something into Being, and creativity is the application of the Creator creating life.

As so far revealed in the preceding chapters the step-by-step journey unfolds:

❖ **From perceiving the focused positive affirmed INTENTION (one).**
❖ **Then listening to the INTUITION (two) channeling "good feelings."**
❖ **Which will open the abundant thought process of the un-manifest CREATIVE (three) Universal Mind.**
❖ **Grounding the negotiated ideas into a "plan of action" through COMMITMENT (four).**
❖ **Accepting TRUST (five) in the process that allows the purpose to be applied in the next step of holding the VISION (six).**

It is from a grounded, committed foundation centered in trusting the journey into the application stage, that the Divine Will is in partnership with the human will releasing the unsure decision making process. It is the path of the practical visionary in the Self on the journey to Understanding through Action, Wisdom and Purpose in the Divine Order of manifesting from right action.

The Creative Mind, in the center of the Conscious Self holds the

Vision through *applying* the Vision. It is at this stage of the Journey (the movie we are making up) that what we have intended begins to be reality in form. It is where we get to see what we are made of!

In creating the movie called My Life it is now time to get out of pre-production and actually start making the movie! Today we begin shooting the movie and the art of Purpose unfolds every day in the movie called *My Life*. Once the step of trust is complete, the vision is now ready to be held in a form called, "Holding the space" of the intention. Through the application of *nurturing* a creation (seed of intention) it will reveal how well we followed the steps leading to actually doing "the work." The work (patience and understanding) will either be displayed in action (thought and deed) as the "lilies of the fields, how they grow; and toil not"—words of Jesus in the Sermon on the Mount—or through self-sacifice and repeated lessons. This aspect will be covered more in Chapter Seven.

Remember pre-production? First, the idea was conceived and then we looked at what it took to make the movie or any aspect of it. Secondly, the script was fine-tuned and the importance of commitment to the project was positively affirmed. We took the process step by step and developed a plan of action, then trusted the intentional idea into a vision of how it *already* felt once manifested— important because it eliminated a future in the "now" of Self-doubt. More importantly, it stabilized the <u>purpose</u> and prevented the *if I only had done* negative affirmed thoughts from occurring. The *if only I had done* happens in the application stage and prevents the Purpose from being completed in the highest vibration of positive affirmed thoughts.

Holding the vision or "holding the space" <u>is</u> the nurturing process.

𝕊 𝕊 𝕊

Imagine shooting a movie and stopping in the middle of a scheduled day with all the cast and crew to say, "Wait a minute. If I had only added another character to this scene, it would make the movie better." Would you stop shooting to go back to the drawing board? Send your actors and crew home for a few weeks while you rethink the scene? Put your project on hold to make it better later? The *only if* process is stuck in the loop of Self-doubt (the personal mind doubting the Self) preventing you from moving any further in your Vision. It means you moved into Trust without making sure you had planned the whole movie out. The Vision then becomes blurred and everything shifts into burden (victim) mode reflecting the *"poor me, if only I had...."* The movie ends up being very costly and the lessons become mirrored in the cast and crew who now doubt your ability to create any Vision successfully.

𝕊 𝕊 𝕊

"Poor me" is the Dangerous Mind sabotaging the Self.

The *practical visionary* values the importance of "holding the vision" in place and has positively affirmed that all the previous steps have been successfully executed.

All is well in my world.

The Faultfinding Worry Warrior

The faultfinder is the critical Dangerous Mind exploiting the weakness of a physical or intellectual imperfection or impairment to an excessive degree. The faultfinder believes there is perfectionism in this world and judges everything and everybody against this standard. The faultfinder withholds an opportunity for excellence in life. For the faultfinder, excellence will not exist because there is always the belief there will be something better.

It is important to connect with how critical we are about anything or anyone. Ask your Self, "Do I find fault with others?" "Is it easy for me to be critical of my Self and my journey?" "Are my expectations of an outcome so high that I can never attain them?"

The faultfinder relies on the blame game. Critical of the Self and others, the faultfinder is forever acknowledging that just for today they have not done the best they could do. There is always something else that should-could-would have been done, something else that has been missed.

The faultfinder is the hall monitor of the worry warriors. The faultfinder creates obstacles for everybody with the *drama of worry* and always holding someone or something responsible.

· *I could do my job better if there weren't so many distractions.*
· *I was in a great mood before the customer started complaining.*
· *I want a loving relationship but every guy is too busy with his job.*
· *My husband watches sports and I do all the chores.*
· *I want to paint but there is not enough room in my house for an easel.*
· *I gave up going to college because I had kids.*
· *How can I be happy with all the problems in the world?*

The faultfinder mirrors the worry in others and reflects anxiety back upon the Self. Whatever the faultfinder tries to do, there is always an excuse why it cannot be done right—the *"I*

can't because . . ."
· *I can't go to the dentist because I can't afford to go.*
· *I can't finish school because my wife says it will be too much of*
   a burden.
· *I can't dance because my feet hurt.*
· *I can't love you because I am afraid of getting hurt.*
· *I can't be honest because I will hurt your feelings.*

The faultfinder costumed as the worry warrior is strong, capable, armored and able to stand up to any obstacle and build a bigger one, defending personal territory to the very last breath while also defending a determined point of view because of a self-destructive and self-sabotaging identity. Whatever self-improvement programs the worry warrior designs are ultimately unattainable and therefore the fault lies in the program, not in the faultfinder. *"Why bother when I will just get lectured for doing it wrong!"*

The field of lower vibrations or negative affirmed thoughts of the faultfinder will attract animate and inanimate sources which will critically mirror/reflect back supporting and verifying the "poor me" attitude, reinforcing what the faultfinder already believes and justifies to be true.

There is a little bit of faultfinder in everyone.

Where does the worry come from? It is something we learn. In the developmental stage of arriving on Earth the first vibration is with family. We observe our parents at work in their lives: the father who strives to support the family by pushing and adjusting to the repeated changes in his position in the world and the mother who is repeatedly anxious over the development of the child, fretting over growth, illness and education. The fretting and the worrying are mental distress and agitation. What mother doesn't say how much she worries about her children's future? What father doesn't worry and fret over whether he will be able to support the family infrastructure on a planet filled with financial insecurity? Fret, worry and lack are "come by honestly" in a world where support is volatile in all governments and resources. Why wouldn't parents worry?

War and famine are seen daily on the news and crisis is the media's little worry pill. Gone are the days of getting under the school desk in case of an atomic war, but not gone are the days of the terrorist attacks. "Don't worry, be happy" may have been the theme of a top ten tune but it is not the motto of any civilization on our planet.

Worry is the subject of persistent or nagging attention or effort to what is the Human progress without Divine attention to the science of being and the art of living.

So the phenomena is reoccurring, passed from one generation to the next, and as the population expands, so does anxiety for just about everything. To deflect the anxious feelings internally, the need to be critical of the external world becomes prevalent.

Worry feeds worry and gives birth to anxiety and fear.

Worry is the measuring stick in the critical over-examination of detail and hearsay. It thrives on fear and dismantles the individual's Beautiful Mind. It destroys the immune system of life and devalues the Soul's place in Human evolution. It makes small all that is enormous and contrives to make petty the journey to Love. Worry is the Dangerous Mind's tool to file away at the spiritual cord that connects to the Higher Self. Worry is lost in the petty details and prevents individuals and societies from understanding the bigger picture, the Universal God-Mind Movie in the making.

- *My mother worried but I am not my mother.*
- *My father fretted over the bills but I am not my father.*
- *The world appears to be in chaos but I am at peace within.*
- *Everything I have been taught is hearsay and not my inner Truth.*

❖ **Make a list of things you worry about and fret over and over again.**
❖ **Who taught you to be a worry warrior?**
❖ **Affirm that you do not have to be the person who taught you, and begin to honor your true Self.**

Discovering the perfection in everything and the excellence in everyone is the journey to connecting to the inner perfection of the Soul. This is the first step to applying the art of joy in the application step of holding a positive affirmed dialogue as the vision to fulfilling any purpose.

Purpose is manifested through the Journey.

❖ **What is your Life Purpose?**
❖ **Do you have Joy in making your Life Purpose?**

Joy in the Application

❖ **How much are you enjoying making your movie?**

Joy is the emotion evoked by well-being, success or good fortune, or by the prospect of possessing what one desires. Joy is a state of happiness that comes from knowing that all is perfect in our world right now. Joy is being okay with who we are today.

Joy unfortunately is attached to perfectionism, which is unattainable, instead of *perfection* exemplified in excellence. If we are not in a state of joy experiencing the journey of life purpose, it is because we are holding perfectionism in the personal mind God box, whether we know it or not!

Joy is choosing our feelings every step of the way. It is taking responsibility for what we feel and how we think about it.

Joy is the barometer of Self-Love.

I have spoken a lot about setting intentions and setting only the ones that allow us to feel good. The feeling good is feeling <u>true</u>. The creative process allows the thoughts to float on while we are feeling true and can be directed by intelligence in the grounded vision of faith—walking the direction of the prayer (desire)—and focused in the Heart-mind. Joy is what we feel in the application of the journey to manifesting the purpose. We can feel good about what we desire but it doesn't stop there within the Law of Attraction. It will only be received for the best and highest good when we are able to feel gratitude that joy is the acceptance of the Gift. Even when the Gift is all lessons created from past unaware/unconscious desires—Law of Cause and Effect—the road least traveled will still be the Universal Journey. Joy allows us to receive all Gifts without judgment and attachment to the world.

Joy is the art of detachment.

Detachment is freedom from bias or prejudice. Accepting joy is the freedom of receiving all Gifts without bias or prejudice.

· *I am too busy to be joyful.*
· *How do I have joy when I don't even have time for myself?*
· *Exactly what do you mean by joy?*
· *How can I be aware of how I feel all the time?*

In the movie of My Life the only reason there are dramatic scenes is because they are placed there for effect. What would happen to our movies if we took out the drama? Without drama could life still be interesting?

Drama is a state, situation, or series of events involving interesting or intense conflict of forces.

Drama is conflict.

There is drama in life because humanity stays in a constant state of conflict. There is drama in our lives because of inner conflicts. As long as there is inner conflict there is a dramatic scene in the making.

Joy lies in knowing that life need not be hard.

In order to remove the drama or the *karmic causes* in life, it is important to first look at what the drama is revealing. It is perhaps the most important part of the journey to purpose thus far. If we have drama in our personal lives it is because there is drama in the inner conflict of the Self. The Self which has yet to know Self-love.

The statement "We are One" has little meaning if its reference is misunderstood. The personal mind does not understand this statement fully because the personal mind is limited by what it believes to be true. Ideas suggesting "Infinite Mind," "Universal Love" and "Peace on Earth" are abstract to the personal mind. We can say such statements but in truth they are meaningless. In order to know such statements as truth, it is first important to understand the statement "We are One." We are not merely made in the image of God but the manifestation of the God-Mind. If action is energy and energy is what the universe is, then we are the action of God in the universe. Every *thing* or form is first energy. We are the universe in all things and form in the Mind of God. Each and every object both animate and inanimate is a form of manifestation and we are of the same material or nature of all things. So when we look out upon the world and universe and all that is within it we can say, "I am that!"

All conflict expressed externally is only a reflection of the Self in conflict with ideas of the Self. Once we know internally, "I am that!" there is the mirror in all things reflecting the oneness of all things in action. Conflict will end when we realize there is no difference between any thing and form. We have all been expressed from the One and will return to the One.

The opportunity to realize that everything is as it should be without reservations held in the limited personal mind will initiate joy into life.

When we truly understand that all judgments (opinions) have been passed down by the storytellers who themselves have been making it all up themselves and are not our personal stories, we can let go of what we think about today and simply en*joy* today. Letting go of all the stories societies teach us about fear and loathing will allow Self-love to express who we really are to the Self. The Self as the manifested One peering out at everything and saying I AM THAT.

Directing with Joy

Everything in our lives is what we create, whether it is drama or joy, hardship or effortlessness. Everyone who is part of our personal universe we have attracted to reflect what we need to understand about that Who We Are is *what we are creating*. If we feel limited, then we are limited. If we feel abundant, then we are abundance expressed. It is difficult sometimes to understand why any lesson has been attracted in the first place. It is because we have attracted it from a limited understanding of what we can receive. First changing how we feel emotionally creates all quantum leaps from the state of faith. Everyone in our lives is here to reflect what changes are required to be made. We attract energy to change our vibration. The better we feel, the greater the change will occur.

In the application stage of making the movie it is a time to place a director who is looking after our best interest. Often the position is given to other people out of a need not to hurt their feelings. At other times it is given to people because of being unable to be responsible enough to the Self to handle the accountability of the project. But the Free Will has many choices in casting the role of director. And the Dangerous Mind believes that no one can make the movie better than itself. Who else can know better what our purpose is than ourselves? Well, if this is true, why are there so many lessons and so much responsibility and burden?

The best director for the movie "My Life" is the Soul—a person's total Self.

Higher purpose is always something we feel as love. The Higher Self knows our Higher Purpose and is the best director in our awareness. It is just a matter of surrendering to what we feel in our

Higher Self and allowing Divine Will to manifest what in truth we desire.

Once we have centered from a place of trust it is time to allow the Higher Director to bring all the necessary parts of the movie together.

After all the time spent in pre-production getting everything ready for the best possible movie why settle for anything less than the best possible director? Now it is time to enjoy the movie of *My Life* in the making, allowing the Abundant Universe to apply all the tools of the trade, all the experience and all the fun. Now is the time for each one of us to have fun participating in *My Life*, the movie, every day. This is the best part of co-creating. We get to do it with the Higher Self!

❖ **Who is directing your movie?**

All of us are required ultimately to take responsibility for what we have created in the past—cause and effect, understanding that all past desires (conscious and unconscious) will manifest at some point. Remaining detached *today* is the key to not reacting emotionally to what has been created in the past—especially if it was created out of fear, reoccurring reactions, anger or distress. Taking responsibility for everything we have created will make it easier to let go of the expressed outcome if we are not holding on to the emotions that were attached to the cause when we created it. Reacting to past-created desires is thinking in *victim mode.* Victims react rather than make conscious choices. Making a conscious choice to not attach emotions *today* to what is being presented and manifested from the past today, as an effect from a past cause, will insure that how we <u>feel</u> today is not associated with how we <u>felt</u> when we set the original intention into motion. If we react today to a past emotionally charged intention,

197

it will attach the same vibration to what we desire (cause) to set into motion in the future (effect). It will then continue to perpetuate past negative affirmed unconscious desires into our future outcomes. The karmic wheel will continue to turn again and again. The more we tap into the joy of our daily life through the application of joy today, the greater the excellence of the movie experience today; all thoughts and desires we are creating today are being created from a place of joy. All future events will arrive in the same state of being in joy. The future will then be perceived as joyful.

Joy rides the wave of the Higher Self.

Joy vibrates as perfect justice. Perfect Justice is the Law of Right Action, the highest vibration in equity with the best and highest good manifested as Divine Order.

Every day we make a conscious effort to tap into joy, the more we will desire nothing less than joy on a daily basis.

In the application stage of creating any purpose it is important to understand it is not what we do in our movies, but who we are in our movies.

Applying the steps from the first six chapters of *Spiritual Bootcamp* we can begin the first day of shooting "doing the work" from a secure foundation centered in trust assuring we can arrive to the purpose of what we have intended. Whether it is a small scene or the movie of life, the journey is the fun part. Having the joyful opportunity to play with all our guest stars, supporting cast and crew—including an incredible director we trust—is the life we want to live. Success in each part of the movie manifests Understanding, Wisdom and Purpose. Imagine what the movie called *My Life* will manifest!

❖ **Who are you becoming?**
❖ **What Intentions can you hand over to the Highest Director of your movie?**

Holding The Vision

Imagine world peace! Well maybe this is reaching too much too soon. So let us take a look at the personal opportunities we have at our disposal to imagine. Whatever we ask for from our heart will manifest.

In previous chapters we have read about the effect the mind has on everything in our lives. If we are having positive affirmed thoughts, we are creating a reality able to appear positive around us…a world where synchronistic happenings take place in our lives—like being in the right place at the right time. The opposite is also true. If we are thinking negative affirmed thoughts and expecting an outcome of anything from a mindset of difficulty, confusion, and divisiveness, the world will mirror the same feelings and thoughts right back.

How important is it to be conscious of what we are thinking?

It is extremely important. Thought is energy in motion and every thought will be realized in some form. If we are thinking bad thoughts about a person it will reflect upon ourselves as bad feelings towards the Self. The universe does not evaporate and simply go away. It contains all that has ever been and ever will be within Universal Mind or God. So it is a matter of consciousness within this Mind that will determine how we perceive what is real or not real. The illusion is that everything we sense with the five senses is real. Well, this is true in part because it is "real" to us since we are making it all up as we go along our paths in this world.

Once we grasp that *we are not our thoughts but the maker of our thoughts* then we can step back a little and ask, "What do I want to create today?" The "what" is the maker of the picture required in the imagination. The thoughts are the tools to visualizing all ideas and are held in the vision of the mind. It is a process of making a new movie in the mind today. It is very much like revising and rewriting to improve upon limited thought patterns we continuously replay to hold what we see in our world everyday. Since we are so busy holding on to the same story everyday, it makes sense that we can also change the story whenever we want.

Our desires are the thoughts we create to make a change in present thinking.

Through the process of *creative visualization,* we can imagine what it is we want to create and then begin to hold the vision in the mind several times a day to change what we have seen as "real" to something new in our reality. It perhaps sounds complicated and may take time to wrap the head around the process but it is actually quite simple to do.

We hold thoughts in the mind both unconsciously and consciously all the time. We perceive certain people in our lives to act and be a certain way everyday. How we hold them in our thoughts is how they act towards us. *Have you ever thought that maybe they are acting differently with others?* If we ask ten people what their impressions are of one certain individual we will hear ten different impressions. No two people hold the same thoughts about the same person! Yes there will be many similarities and ways to compare but this usually happens after the individual talked about has been shared with each other. We are holding thoughts about our careers, relationships, prosperity and health in the same way and making assumptions about how nothing has changed very much from day to day.

Holding these thoughts in such a manner is exactly what holds such reality in check. Limited beliefs and notions about how everything is supposed to be and act are held in our personal reality. This personal reality is an illusion. Nothing remains the same; only the intention we hold on to is the same and stagnates us. There is an opportunity to reinvent what we want fresh and new each day if we are willing to begin by using creative visualizations twice a day.

Since thought is energy, all we need to do is place certain thoughts in the mind. When we begin to concentrate on new thoughts we will connect electrically charged positive affirmed ideas into action. The brain does not know the difference between what is symbolic and what is "real." Therefore the new thoughts will initiate an energy field upon the ideas in the mind and see them as real. Remember we are part of the Universal Mind Power, or God, so whatever we begin to entertain in our mind's eye begins to materialize.

When we begin to change our thoughts we begin to change the way the mind looks at our perception of reality. By rewriting the script we begin to release the habitual mindset of previous thoughts and actions. We begin to tap into a different world than the one we keep repeating in our thoughts.

This is not the material world around that we are changing but our own thoughts about the world we live in each day.

Some thoughts are difficult to change. We have held certain limited ideas in space for a very long time and it will take time for certain ways of thinking and acting to change. Be assured that with time the changes will take place, so it is important not to become disappointed if the changes are not fitting into our present time schedule. Simply continue to hold the vision of "what you want" to change, and meditate and visualize this everyday. This is where patience and faith are our greatest reward.

Creative visualizations are first imagined. When we think of what it is we want to change in life, it is important to write the thoughts down. Afterwards read what is written and modify the story with as many details as can be added. See, smell, taste, feel and hear the story in the mind's eye—the center of the imagined world. Once the story is as full and robust as can be imagined, rewrite the story from a point of view that it has *already* happened. In other words, place the story in the past, perhaps six months or a year ago and remember it with a great feeling of accomplishment and success. It is even better if it is read to someone close and give it energy by telling it like a great storyteller. See how well they respond to it before telling them it has yet to be manifested!

Now that the story has been placed on paper and has a sense of reality about it in nature, begin to read it over and over again at least twice a day throughout the weeks. While reading it feel good about it and remember how good it was when it came true. Remember, it is important to see the story as already true even if the present "reality" appears to be different. A vivid imagination is how dreams come true.

Creative visualizations are related to dreams. In dreams we are already in the time and place of the dream and everything appears real to us. This is what will be required from the storyteller's perception. The time and effort placed on this process will be well worth the time spent imagining a new reality.

When we imagine ourselves inside the place we have created in our mind, we also are required to sit quietly for five or ten minutes a day visualizing our new world.

฿ ฿ ฿

❖ Write down the imagined story as if it has already come true.

❖ Detail the story as much as possible. See yourself in the story.

❖ Read the story out loud to your Self and then repeat it to a friend.

❖ Sit quietly twice a day in preparation for the creative visualization.

❖ Relax and quiet your breathing to place the body in light meditation.

❖ Begin visualizing the story in your imagination. If any part has been left out then simply open your eyes and read the story your Self.

❖ Feel good about the story you have created and how much happiness it has brought you right now.

❖ Let the Spirit-Mind-Body connect to the imagined story.

❖ After the meditation is completed thank the Universal Mind or God within for making it so.

฿ ฿ ฿

It is important to continue this practice daily. If what we want to create is important and has value to others it will also have value to us. Whenever creating an imagined story it is important to understand the value of having only positive affirmed thoughts when creating the details of the story. Always have positive thoughts.

A lot of words have been placed on positive thinking but it is also important to remember that positive thoughts alone are not enough. It is also important to remember where the positive thoughts are created. It is in conscious awareness we know that all thoughts we are thinking manifest from Source as the maker of thoughts. From this awareness we realize we are not our thoughts at all. Whenever we have already imagined what we want to create, it is with gratitude and thanks to the Universal Mind, the God Source within each of us, which is first expressing all that we imagine from the infinite imagined mind of God.

I often remind myself that the God Source within me has already known what it is I want and by the time I am thinking about it and asking for it, the thing I want has already been manifested in time and space. The Higher Consciousness of Who I Am has always held the vision.

Discovery

1. What are you striving to attain?

2. What do you believe Divine Will to be?

3. Make a list of things you constantly worry and fret over.

4. Who taught you to be a worry warrior?

5. Affirm that you do not have to be the person who taught you, but honor your Self.

6. What is your Life Purpose?

7. Do you have Joy in making your Life Purpose?

8. How much are you enjoying making your movie?

9. Who is directing your movie?

10. Who are you becoming?

11. What Intentions can you hand over to the Highest Director of your movie?

12. Develop a creative visualization by writing a story from a point of view that it has already happened. Visualize the story twice a day in a state of light meditation.

Everyday Affirmations

My mother _____ but I am not my mother.

My father _____ but I am not my father.

The world appears to be in chaos but I am at peace within.

Everything I have been taught is hearsay and not my inner Truth.

I am exchanging my thoughts for new thoughts everyday.

Compassion is sometimes the fatal capacity for feeling what it is like to live inside somebody else's skin. It is the knowledge that there can never really be any peace and joy for me until there is peace and joy finally for you too.

- Frederick Buechner

Chapter 7

Understanding Is the Mystery

Everything Occurs for a Purpose

The meaning of understanding is to interpret, in one of a number of possible ways, the experiences of the journey. On the road to purpose, and the final manifestation realized from intention, it is trust in the heart, without utter certainty, that will lead to the wisdom from action. It is the knowing more than we believe we know through the journey of direct and shared experiences.

From holding the vision to ultimate purpose, understand that everything occurs for a purpose and can only occur in the art of learning through individual involvement. It is from grounding on the Mental Plane Conscious Self process of application through the inner knower of *all that* is necessary; this is known as "doing the Work."

Whatever the work is, even if it is a simple task or a larger life purpose, it is at this deeper understanding through experience that we begin to know what the work is and then simply do the work. It lies in understanding that the work is for the Highest Good on the journey to manifesting purpose.

Once the intention has evolved through the step-by-step process of intuition, followed by negotiation into clarity, commitment and planning, faith and trust, application with attainable goals, it then becomes necessary to *understand the issues in order to transcend them.*

The direct experience of the work is understood through the art of trial and error without shame, guilt or secrecy as well as being intimate and open to trust with a childlike heart. Hence, it is being open and willing to experience everything without judgment in the patient process of creation.

Understanding is connecting to the depth of the inner experience.

Allowing the work to develop through vision creates the optimum journey in the *depth* of the experience and not just simply the *breadth* of it. But oftentimes this is the jumping off point for many people. It is the point where the fear of the energy being experienced blocks the willingness of the mind to dive deeper into the Inner Knower. Thus, this often leads a person to think they have been satisfied enough and need not go any deeper. It is the journey's end for the internal seekers.

The internal seekers will only allow a certain level of trust from the advice or experiences of others. He or she will bounce from one experience to another failing to learn from other people's experiences and often from their own. They will always look for the next teacher, mentor, guru or advisor's counsel without ever including their own inner truths to blend with their wisdom.

The internal seeker fails to learn from other people's experiences.

Any deep understanding will evolve once the internal seeker allows the process of trial and error to blend with the experiences of everything and everybody. All experiences are aspects of love. However, the internal seeker will seek advice only to ignore other people's ideas due to a limited faith in their own inner resources, or oftentimes they will only trust other people's models believing it will work for them.

The internal seeker will believe that deeper philosophical knowing comes from the understanding of the Mental Self and need not be understood in the grounding opportunity of the work.

Oftentimes internal seekers are the first to say they trust themselves, but mainly they trust what their personal minds thinks without being aware that Self-trust is *an inner process behind an external achievement.*

The internal seeker does not believe everything happens for a purpose.

The Dangerous Mind is always telling the internal seeker the only way to understand anything is through personal direct experience, but does not include that this kind of experience becomes the most memorable when it involves personal self-sacrifice. The Dangerous Mind relies on the Conscious Self and fails to connect to the deeper philosophical understanding that assists in learning without repeating the lessons. And so the experiences, developing to purpose, are short-lived and a new experience replaces one direct experience for another. Thus, the lessons are repeated again and again.

Hoarding the Light

Breaking through to align with the Higher Self can oftentimes be more about stumbling on the path of understanding the world around us. It can be difficult to open up and share our experiences with other people because of deeper feelings about abandonment, guilt, shame and past betrayals. Sharing or exchanging ideas might have led to hurt, thus creating blocks to any trust of others and to the Self. Sometimes listening to others and following their paths, instead of our own, will leave us feeling helpless after they have left us to our own devices. This stumble becomes the fall into shame.

The shame game, much like the blame game, reflects the painful emotions caused by past programs of guilt or shortcomings connected to personal identity. Both feelings leave us struggling in the Conscious Self and we wind up picking up the pieces of our life. Sometimes the trust in the Self is mirrored by how much trust is given to others who have betrayed our trust, therefore leaving us feeling a lower vibration (negative affirmed thoughts) of shame for having been blind to such manipulation of feelings. Losing a sense of trust in others turns into the issue of not being able to be trustworthy to the Self. Outer expressions turn inward for Self-examination and often to Self-doubt.

Unable to share feelings connected to trust, the doubter believes any intimate expression will cause pain and turns inward to hoard the Light once shared with others. If at anytime the issues of personal intimacy are already in place, hoarding the Light becomes easier than before.

Intimacy starts in the childlike heart of a person who trusts others to nurture, protect and love in reflection. If love as "in the name of love" has been bartered or hoarded by parents who have known deep shame themselves, or a lack of personal intimacy with others, the childlike heart becomes squandered. Intimacy is not shared openly because love has become a very personal or private affair of the heart, and not easily given or received. Love becomes impersonalized and the childlike heart learns to hoard the Light—hiding it in a box—at a very young age.

Children in their sensitive nature learn fast that love is not given freely as desired, but hoarded because of lessons from personal self-sacrifice having been repeated too many times.

When a child arrives on this planet they are open to receive and to give love. At an early age the world around them does not reflect an open and willing desire to share, so the child sometimes makes an unconscious choice, at once keeping it to him- or herself or burying it in the backyard thereby hiding his or her Light where no one can harm it. As the years roll by they believe they can live in this world without the Light and the Inner Knower seems to fade away. Never having the requirement to share the Light with the world, the child grows up and the childlike heart is replaced with the only trust they believe they will ever need: to trust no one, eventually forgetting where they buried their Light.

Squandered and forgotten the multi-faceted Self moves through Life on a journey of more self-sacrifice, affirming that the needs of others should be placed above their own. All the lessons of love are then repeated over and over again eventually teaching through the art of sharing or the lessons of living a secret life.

❖ **How many ways can I share my Light with the others?**

The Gristmill to Gratitude

Many times the Journey to gratitude can only be understood from the process of life through a gristmill. All the lessons are turned around and around until the understanding becomes the advantage, resulting from some course of action evolving mistakes into benefits. But the gristmill is the hard grind. The hard lessons are ground over a period of time to *refine* the deeper understanding, and sometimes the lessons appear very hard.

Working things out on a gristmill of gratitude sometimes seems to be the hardest thing to do. However, when the journey is to repeat a lesson again and again through the intensified process of learning, it often results in feeling the goal to purpose is all but unattainable from the struggle. Gratitude like appreciation becomes overwhelmed by a constant sense of failures.

Then why insist on creating the hard lessons?

The difficulty lies in understanding the issues and then transcending them. For whatever reason the question becomes *Why me?* instead of *What is the issue that repeats itself?* It is important to release the *why* and focus on the *what*. The *why* can originate from a myriad of reasons. It can be from lack of Self-worth to lack of trust, or most of the time it is the constant impatience with the process of trial and error. The *what* connects to the analytical aspect of the Mental Conscious Self and then processes the information by Self-examination. Self-trust needs to be an ingredient of self-examination. Without respect to loving the Self the examination turns to self-ridicule and lack of understanding the necessary steps required to positive affirmed thoughts in action.

When mistakes are understood as simply changes in the growth of consciousness leading to greater awareness, it becomes easier to examine the issues that have led to repeating the same mistakes. But when mistakes are negatively affirmed as error due to fault, wrong-doing and shame, it is harder to be open to understanding ways of rectifying past lessons and moving beyond them.

Mistakes are often viewed as problems that require fixing. Mistakes are simply *changes in the growth towards higher consciousness* but are oftentimes viewed as signs of wrongdoing or bad decisions. A mistake in and of itself should not be connected to any emotionally charged thought process. The *censors* in the personal mind attribute to feelings connected to past programs in the identity, but unfortunately this is usually not the case. Mistakes are connected to past errors and the retributions following any mistake may have consequences reflecting on the person who made the mistake. Unfortunately mistakes become deemed as "poor judgments" and seen as foolishness and stupidity which in turn can attach to a person's feelings of incompetence. If we are *already* in our imagination having thoughts connected to lack of self-esteem and self-worth the power of past programs or experiences intensifies. It is therefore important to view all mistakes as opportunities of growth and understanding without passing judgment on the incident or situation. Mistakes can bring the best and worst out in people simply because society at large has been programmed to believe people are waiting and observing a person to point out their failures even to laugh at them. The positive affirmed person knows this is not true. This perspective is usually only an internal program in the individual because of thinking the world will find out they are incompetent in the first place, barely holding their own in business, relationships and education. The truth of the matter is once we shift to the maker of our thoughts instead of believing we are our thoughts we realize most of the time the world is viewing us from a place of prompting us to higher successes in life. People are attracted to successful people and ultimately are unhappy around negatively and emotionally charged people.

❖ **Do I Trust in the process of Self-examination?**

Consider for a moment lessons as obstacles. Then examine what may be the reasons for the lessons and what they are really expressing and showing us. If desires are not in balance or alignment with the beliefs being held, the journey to the desired outcome will feel like the stress from pushing a rock uphill. But in actuality the journey is in retrograde, only appearing to be moving along a downhill climb walking backwards!

For example, an intention is set for a certain outcome but the resulting action can only be manifested if it happens in a certain way. Something first must happen before allowing the intention to be placed in motion. The *something first* is another or previous intention. The previous intention is set into motion only to discover that it can only happen if done in a certain way too! The *something first* has its own *something* required in order for it to be created before allowing it to be set into motion. The cycle goes on and on as we move farther backwards down the hill creating yet another intention with yet another *something* that must occur before it can also be manifested.

By the time the process is complete we are at the bottom of the hill looking up at the mound of intentions, now appearing to be a huge set of obstacles piled on top of each other. It is not that the mound feels unattainable but something more insurmountable. What was once an intention has now become many intentions contingent on each other before *anything* can happen. It is a reverse pyramid effect and we feel we are back where we started, looking at the original intention perplexed and asking *why*?

All the possibilities would take an enormous amount of self-sacrifice, but determination to have what we want at no cost will force the climb back up the hill to get whatever it was we first intended. Each contingent intention has to be conquered before moving to the next intention and so on.

For many people the personal experience is found in only doing it the hard way and it must have a personal sacrifice involved to be memorable. They do not see any opportunity in getting what they want without doing it themselves.

The personal self-sacrifice of learning through the experience must be made in order to feel able to teach and share. Doing it the hard way, creating as many obstacles as possible, reinforces the belief of limited faith and insures that no intuition is necessary to get what they want. It is all created from shear *will* and determination to finish the goal. And, it is gained and sacrificed for no matter what the cost to them. It is the gristmill of strong determination and a willful intention to drive forward even if it means going backwards all the way!

If they are not able to succeed or are unable to finish, it is with personal shame they will then recede back into the cavern of their lives, not for self-examination, but to hide their guilt from the world in secret.

These repeated lessons eventually become the Gift and eventually drive a person to dig deeper into the forces behind the circumstances opening them into self-examination.

Understanding the nature of obstacles begins with letting go of Self-doubt.

Shame reflects shortcomings and mirrors a lack of Self-trust. If we are operating from an inability to share our conflicts with others due to fear of intimacy, then the opportunity to be open becomes the obstacle of Self-sacrifice. It is necessary then to discover our ability to connect with the inner knower. The inner knower knows more than we believe.

However, tapping into the breadth of the mind is the *internal seeker*. It is how the connection is possible for those operating from an unwillingness to be intimate with others. It is the path of least resistance, and unwittingly, it appears to be the best opportunity for attaining Highest Good.

The Inner Knower opens the channels for discovering what we doubt in our Self and in other people. It allows forgiveness of Self for trusting naively and being hurt by others and, most of all, by hurting the Self within. The Inner Knower speaks from wisdom and compassion telling us that it is okay to release the hurt we allowed our Self to receive, whether that hurt came from the intentional lack of knowing Self-love or from being naive in trusting others without creating necessary boundaries. The Inner Knower offers us the opportunity to share what cannot be shared with anyone else.

The Inner Knower integrates Intuition with Trust to remove Self-doubt.

The Self-sacrifices we create in our lives become the compassion we understand about life itself. There would be no need for any sacrifices if there is the understanding that fear of the energy of life is what we are unwilling to release. Fear of energy, the dynamic spiritual Force that excels us into the Highest Good and flows from our deepest desires to know Transparent Love, needs no reflection. But as it is easy to say, it is not so easy to understand without expressing negatively affirmed doubts and openly revealing and transcending them. It is through the practical expression of blending our sixth sense, or intuitive ESP with our common sense allows this to occur. It is the Inner Knower in balance without expectations with the conscious mind.

When the conscious mind *expects* to create, and fuels the desires in the Human Will, it manifests as lessons in daily life. Through personal experiences we begin to understand the lessons and gradually the lessons will no longer be repeated. It is a philosophical understanding that being calm or unflinching in the face of trouble, defeat, or loss—reflected in the gristmill of the lessons—prevents the reactive or victim mode shutting down the process by failing to comprehend what the lessons are expressing.

Calm is a state of tranquility without reservations.

Tranquility manifests when we connect to the Inner Knower and work things out on the gristmill with affirmations of appreciation and gratitude.

Gratitude is thankfulness and being conscious of the benefits received utilizing positive affirmed thoughts everyday. The benefits are the rewards from the hardship of the gristmill. They are the refined, subtle aspects that have been reduced from the totality of the grist, the grains that have come forth from the seeds of our intentions. It is in the refining of the grains sewn by unconscious and unaware intentions that have been created *not* in the Highest and Best Good. This refining defines the experiences on the journey through trial and error that lead us to connecting to the deeper understanding of the journey.

As the Seeds of Intentions are refined the Inner Knower is revealed.

Understanding the art of refinement, which blossoms from trial and error, is the revelation of the grounding of Gratitude and the understanding manifested *in everything*.

Being grateful is being content with *Who I Am* every moment. It is not just saying *I'm grateful* for something given or received, but also simply *knowing that I already know*.

· *I am grateful for being here right now.*
· *I am grateful for being still.*
· *I am grateful for each step I create and each stop I take.*
· *I am grateful for the silence.*
· *I am grateful for the lessons learned.*

· *I am grateful for today.*

❖ **What am I grateful for today?**

Compassion Is Without Shame

It is easy to say "I can be sympathetic to others' pain and their forbearance of intolerance" until the mirror reflects. It becomes even more difficult to be sympathetic to pain and forbearance of intolerance when the act of being compassionate is to be patient with suffering and sympathetic to the sufferer when it is our Self.

The Higher Self is always present to relieve the urgency of pain. The very nature of being compassionate is the desire to relieve all burdens of the sufferer.

❖ **What do you believe your Higher Self wishes for you?**

Patience with the suffering of others impacts because often the suffering of others reflects the inner conflicts of the observer. Feelings of guilt arise from the observer feeling incapable of doing anything to help. The feelings of helplessness and fear of shame often lead the observer to a state of avoidance. The essence of suffering is always an opportunity to understand what the other person is experiencing and then helping in a way that relieves the pressure of suffering is Divine compassion. Everyone experiences the nature of suffering at some point and it is in this suffering that we discover how much we are willing to *share.*

It is the nature of suffering that leads to understanding the nature of sharing.

The inability to share is an inner conflict within the *internal seeker's* negative affirmed thoughts of shame, guilt or unconscious fears of rejection. Sharing is intimate, as is suffering— the opposite of joy—and intimacy like joy requires nurturing. Even though both pain and joy are polar opposites, each reside in the human heart. Embracing both unites us in our deepest understanding of the human journey through sacrifice. In failing to learn from others' experiences we are destined to repeat the same lessons.

Shame exists because of hoarding the Light. Once we understand purpose through the experience and progress of Self, no matter how small the experiences, life is deepened through sharing the Light with everything and everyone.

I am the Divine Light Within.

Comprehending and understanding this affirmation applies to everyone, even if we do not believe it! The Highest Good is only understood when we are One in the Divine Light including those who are suffering the most. This is true of even those who appear to be behaving in a manner that is observed as "evil." All is judgment or opinion and mirrored in the shame of not being able or willing to help them on either side of the same spiritual path. It is often easier to just simply ignore them and retreat inward. It always appears easier to love the ones that are easy to love and ignore the ones who the hardest to love.

Ignored is what is not understood.

Intimacy and Opening To Trust

Intimacy is feigned in the solitary life. Sometimes what we feel is so deeply felt that it appears to be impossible to share it with anyone else. If at some point it has been shared and rejected, or even belittled, it is difficult to share again. Often the deepest feelings are the hardest to express in words, and when spoken feel shallow and meaningless—not necessarily to the observer, but to the Self. The inner conflict of a need to express what is felt is suppressed by the greater need to be inwardly private.

Growing up in a family who never expresses how they feel but only say what is expected, mirrors the growing anguish in the childlike heart. The Inner Soul Child is asking for honesty and truthfulness, but instead is given reasons and justifications, or logic and ideas for why real feelings should never be expressed.

The Light gets buried in the backyard and remains there often for a very long time. It may take years before the longing to know real love brings the solitary Self out of a cave to discover what has been lost so many years ago.

But where is the Light buried? And does it still shine?

The solitary Self begins to express the inner loneliness, and silently shouts *I Am Here*!

Dorothy, in the *Wizard of Oz*, journeyed for miles through dangerous worlds with her three graces—a tin man without a heart, a scarecrow without a brain, and a lion without courage—and hand in hand they traveled in search of what they desired for their own Self and each other. They imagined all would get what each wished for the most. Their desire to have what would make them whole outweighed all the obstacles placed in front of them.

What they discovered along the way is what each one believed they personally lacked, the others believed they did not lack anything at all. Each solitary Self became shared in a common purpose. First it was to understand and embrace what they did not believe was in fact true and, secondly, they shared the journey of discovering this common truth with each other. At the end of the yellow brick road the journey appeared to be coming to an end. Whatever the truth may be they were ready to know. Along the journey they each shared their deepest regrets and happiness and discovered, in turn, their shared Self. It no longer mattered what was at the end of the road because what they discovered along the road was what they already *had within* and was never aware of. They realized they where whole, happy and always home and just did not know it. They felt deeper than they knew they had felt because the spiritual tools required for the journey were already present within each of them. It no longer mattered what they would receive at journey's end, because the journey was the realization of the desire fulfilled.

The journey was all they created together before entering into a new chapter of their lives. They said heartfelt "good-byes" to each other and spoke their last farewells. Dorothy awakened from the dream surrounded by all she had thought was gone in her life and became aware in that very instant that nothing truly loved, nothing wished upon a star, or imagined in the heart is ever far away. The metaphor speaks of having to look no farther than our own backyard—the Self expressed from the God within.

The Inner Knower whispers that we do not have to look any further than the Heart or center of Universe within.

❖ **What does your Heart whisper to you?**

Whatever the reasons for hiding the Light or hoarding the Light and wherever it is believed to have been misplaced, to find it is as easy as closing our eyes, taking a deep breath, and clicking our heels three times. Open your eyes and be free.

· *Once for Peace.*
· *Once for Wisdom.*
· *And always for Love.*

Discovery

1. **How many ways can I share my Light with the others?**

2. **Do I Trust in the process of Self-examination?**

3. **What am I grateful for today?**

4. **What do you believe your Higher Self wishes for you?**

5. **What does your Heart whisper to you?**

Everyday Affirmations

I will share more of myself with me.

I am open to learning from other's experiences.

All feeling of shame I release to God within.

I see the Divine Light within me every time I look in the mirror.

Becoming more patient with my pain allows me to be more patient with other people's pain.

I am compassionate towards myself.

Loving my Self fully is the first step in loving others.

I am grateful for all I receive and I am willing to share myself with others.

As I understand more deeply I transmute shame and guilt to Love.

Life begets life. Energy creates energy. It is by spending our Self that one becomes rich.

- Sarah Bernhardt

Chapter 8

The Bigger Picture

We Are Not Born Knowing
What Life Has To Offer

We arrive from the Celestial and become Terrestrial to know the Wisdom in the Unity of both. The journey begins and our suitcase is invisible, yet it carries the wealth and abundance of the Universe within. Like the Fool card in the Tarot representing the symbol of zero, we stand on the precipice of the world exuberantly experiencing life with each leap of faith to master our heroic journey. The zero represents the *grace* within God-Self or unmanifest Universe accompanying us along the road—or film reel—of time. The zero symbolically represents expansion. All that "Is" is becoming all the "Is" always desired to be. We are supported in our endeavors whether we believe it or not. Opportunity and good fortune are our companions and the Inner Knower is our guide.

I have wondered how some people seemingly know what they will do here on Earth and how others, like myself, have absolutely no idea! I pondered this question for many years and one night in a dream the answer was revealed to me with a laugh track included. The voice joyfully announced, "You checked the box before you came!" I thought, *What box*? And the words were sung back to me. "The box you selected read, '*I want life to be a surprise!*'"

Why did I want it to be a surprise? I immediately knew the answer. Because it is the kind of person I AM! And then I heard, "So did everybody else!" And more laughter followed.

Some place in my Self I know the journey is forever and that this life I am having here on Planet Earth is an experience and expression—through a sequence of opportunities I have traveled to many countries. Interestingly enough, even as a boy I knew I would travel places I loved and had a passion about. I chose Italy for the food, the Renaissance art and the language. I chose Japan for the cultivated and manicured beauty, and I chose Earth probably in the same way. Sometimes I think the enticement to come here was for the chocolate! (Laughter track.)

But I know I chose this magnificent planet because it is so green and blue. And I also chose it because it mirrors the Universal Abundance in the Diversity of people, wildlife and cultures! For whatever reason the final truth is I know it is wonderful place to grow.

❖ Why did you choose to come here?

Many people believe we are here to go to school, that life is all about "lessons" and learning. Some people think we are here to figure out some great mystery, or to be saved. Many people believe we have no choice, that life is some great exhale and we just showed up to do whatever it is we are going to do, be served whatever we are given and to make the best of it. No matter what we believe, the one thing for sure is that we are *born without knowing what life has to offer.*

The journey of understanding is simply living every day—thinking we know what we are doing at this moment, planning what we are going to do next and knowing that we do not really have any control over anything past, present or future.

Do we have choices through vision?

Is it actually possible to know what is coming, at least to some degree? One thing is for certain: We know we are going to stop breathing one day and say "good-bye" to this world. But is there a possibility we can know even more than this?

Sure, there is the daily routine, much like in the movie *Groundhog Day*, where we wake up each morning and begin the same routine we have most every day: eat breakfast, bathe, go to work, school or take care of chores. Then every night we watch the television programs at certain times, or whatever is the nightly activity in our households—the recurring daily life.

Certain things always seem to consist of the same things every day.

But what if today I wake up and say to my Self, "This is the last day I will be alive on this planet." Then what might happen?

§ § §

❖ **What would you do today if this were the last day you were here on Earth?**

What would you do differently? What if there was a catastrophic event in your life today? What if you died today?

§ § §

I died once.

I left a vehicle after it flipped eight times on a narrow highway on the Amalfi Coast in Italy. I was in the front passenger seat: the "death seat." I was accompanying two friends to Napoli after a weekend in Positano and we were driving the Amalfi Coast—a cliff side highway that is a very narrow and extremely dangerous hairpin curved road. My dear friend driving the car lost control and swerved slamming us

232

into the side of a mountain. My other friend was asleep in the back seat of the car when it happened. None of us were wearing seat belts at the time.

I remember the car beginning to swerve out of control and, like a bullet, it moved directly for the side of the mountain. I remember, just before we hit it, placing both my hands on my face and saying out loud, "This is it!"

The next few moments moved in slow motion. The car began to flip over and over again. My body banged on the ceiling and then on the seat over and over again. I believe it was at least eight or nine times. I heard the tape player ironically blasting *Whip It* by the group Devo. And then all at once I felt my body leave the car. I went through the windshield, except there wasn't any glass left to stop me. Free, and with a sense of slow motion I went through the air and eventually skidded on the concrete highway. Later I was told the only piece of clothing I had left on my body was one shoe, all the rest of my clothes were shredded off my torso.

Then there was silence. I have no idea how long I laid there before I opened my eyes, but when I finally did it was dark and it was very quiet at two o'clock on Monday morning on this particular highway. With my eyes opened I tried to move, but I could not move my body. I felt warm and somehow knew it was from the blood coming out of my body from where there had once been skin.

I laid there in the silence, certain that I was only somewhat alive. And in my mind I waited for the "white light." Yes, I had been studying such phenomena since I was very young. While I waited I began thinking about all the things I wished I could do at that very moment. So many thoughts flashed before my mind's eye. One of the multitudes of thoughts I was having came as a picture of my Mother. At the time she was home in Texas on a Sunday doing her usual chores with the television on in the background to keep her company, I imagined. I saw her in her routine, the one she always had on Sundays. I thought how much I wished I had a telephone so I could call her. I wanted to call her and tell her how much I loved her. I wanted to tell her not to worry to or be upset. I wanted to say that everything was okay and that, as far as I could tell, I wasn't in any pain. I wanted her to know that my life had been wonderful, and that I would miss her and I would watch over her.

I thought of my friends, who were in the car with me, and I tried to shout out their names, but I could not speak. I then told *everybody I ever knew that I loved them* and that I would always love them no matter where I went.

I did not think about anyone who I might have shared pain, or sorrow or regret with in life. I did not think about my work or my financial debt or my career. I only thought about how much I was going to miss my friends and family. I thought about how much I loved them and how much I loved the world.

How do you measure your wealth without Life?

And then I saw the "white light." Once again I thought to myself, *this is it*!

But it wasn't the Light I thought it should be. It was the light of automobiles stopping and people running up to me on the highway and screaming. I heard their screaming and it rang in my ears and I thought, *I must look pretty bad*!

And then I went unconscious.

From that moment forward, I would come in and out of consciousness. I remember being in an ambulance sitting on the *side* watching and observing the paramedics work on my body. My body was a bloody mess and yet they continued to shock my chest. The next moment I was simply 360-degree awareness. I was aware that

I Am no different in this "place" as I was before the accident, I was aware that the only difference was I had stopped breathing. I was the same wherever I was in or out of the physical conscious awareness. I knew *I am still present.*

I was in a hospital on an operating table split wide open while several doctors held my organs in their hands and again blood was everywhere. I watched them as they placed disks on my chest and my body jumped erratically. I watched, and I observed, as if I were watching someone else going through the drama. I watched and I asked for grace in my mind's eye.

A few weeks later I awakened in more than one state of consciousness. To me it seemed as if it had been only a few moments. Time meant nothing and I would not realize, for many days to come, how long I had been in and out of a coma. When I first opened my eyes I was lying down in a hospital bed, in traction, hanging like a puppet on strings. I opened my eyes several times during the course of my stay but again with no sense of time. Each time I regained consciousness, I remembered thinking I had been somewhere else but I now only felt the *presence* of the memory and that *I was safe* in the presence.

For a long time it had all felt like a dream. When I was awake I was in the hospital. When I was unconscious I was someplace safe. It went back and forth like that for weeks.

It wasn't for sometime that I learned my friends had died in the car accident. It was a much longer time later that I was told I had been brought back to life and that I had been in a coma for several days. I never told anyone I already knew everything that had occurred. For me it all seemed like a few minutes at the most. Time had simply stopped. It had only been a few moments in my life.

I went through a long recovery that lasted for many months.

Afterwards I spent many more months learning how to walk again. I had to be weaned off of all the drugs they had given me. I had been in horrible pain from back injury, broken bones and cracked hips, suffering terribly in the last few months of recovery. The pain was so bad, even on morphine, that I would wail and cry through the night. It would be a long time before I would be able to begin my personal journey of grieving for the loss of my two friends who died that night so long ago.

The doctors said time would heal my wounds, but I did not believe it then. I felt I would never be healed. The event that had taken place would change my life forever. I knew I was not the same person that I had been before the accident.

Little did I know, years later, I would be glad that I was not the same person. After that night, so long ago, I would feel something I had never really felt before. I would forever appreciate the life I have here and now.

If I had to go back and do it all again, knowing what I know now, I would get back in that car!

We awake every day, sometimes to the same routine. We eat breakfast, go to the office, school or start chores. On the weekend, we relax with family or friends.

❖ **How much do you appreciate all that you have?**

Catastrophic events often happen in people's lives to shock them into the deeper feelings and the profound meaning of life and higher awareness. The events or situations may occur to create an awakening to the Inner Knower and to offer alternate paths in life that appeared unavailable before.

For me, the event occurred to awaken me to the Gifts I had *before*

I came to this planet. So far I have had an incredible journey. Up until the accident I had traveled the world and indulged in everything I believed life had to offer. The key word is "indulged" because it was a life of self-gratification. What I did not know before was that life was offering me so much more than all the trimmings I had limited myself to enjoyment because of my limited belief system. It was offering me the chance to awaken to the *inner* possibilities of life. The freedom I searched for could never be found outside of myself and certainly not on a planet filled with a population that has never known real freedom. The freedom now truly available to me was the *inner* journey of Self-awareness. That journey I had yet to take.

❖ **What catastrophic events are taking place right now on Earth?**

I never really felt safe here and I never believed that life was any more than an exploration of the mind and body. If I had a Soul, it was something intangible. My heart was ruled by my personal mind and, whether I knew it or not, also by negative affirmed programming that I began to receive after birth.

My catastrophic event was to shock me into connecting with what I only thought existed and had never felt I *knew*. The event shocked me into having *extended perception* and *transcendental power.* Little did I know then how much life really has to offer!

What does Life have to offer you?

After a few weeks in the hospital a nurse came into my room and plugged in a phone. She looked at me and smiled. She said I had a phone call and handed me the phone. It was my Mother calling to say how much she loved me.

Developing Appreciation

In making the movie called *My Life*, every small and large intention taken step by step from the nine stages initialized with positive affirmed thoughts and journeyed to developing understanding includes two more stages. In the eighth stage it is important to elevate the activity of forming a partnership with the Conscious-Mind/ Conscious-Emotional Self through developing appreciation for everything in life that has led us to experiencing our Heart's Desire through manifestation of <u>purpose</u>. Before purpose may be expressed fully—alignment of thoughts and desires—it is valuable to gain the WISDOM derived from the co-creation taking place between the God-Self (infinite possibility) within and the spirit-mind-body of our Self.

Nothing ever happens without the help of others, whether they are our planetary co-creators, assistants, helpers, or cheerleaders. Even more so, it is important to recognize the universe for all the abundance we allow our Self to receive in the process.

For some people it appears easy. If they are born with a silver spoon in their mouths, they already know they have abundance from birth. *Really?* It is not to say that the journey for them cannot be very difficult because they may have to learn how to keep it. For everyone else the knowledge of what the universe is readily offering may not be so apparent. The journey can be a struggle in understanding what the entire process is all about.

I have shared with you in previous chapters how important it is *not to miss any steps on the path* to purpose because of the anxieties that will manifest, creating fear through the failure to believe we will succeed in the journey of our hearts.

Life is hard until we figure out that it actually is difficult and then decide to make it as easy on our Self as we can. Oftentimes the hardest part is figuring out this very thing! But when we are making our big life movies or just small episodes every week or more, it is important to remember all of the people who have helped and shared with us in the movie-making process. It is sort of like the motion picture awards, except we are not limited to three minutes. We can take all the time we please in expressing how deeply heart felt we are for all the support.

It is something that is overlooked more often than not. In general, we often feel that others already know they are appreciated and we do not need to say it. What happens is the *often*, becomes *once in awhile* and sometimes, *never*! If we cannot remember the last time friends, family and co-workers were thanked—cast, crew and guest players in our movies—or how much we appreciate them, it may be we believe we are *independent of everyone else.*

Being independent usually means a fear of being dependent. It actually means that the mirror reflected back at us is waxing and waning between the desires of feeling independent, yet oftentimes more dependent than we wish to believe. In telling others how much their support and their provisions created our ability to manifest what is desired, *we share in the prosperity, the abundance of the intention.*

If we find it difficult to express appreciation it is because of fear of giving up control. Sort of like being the boss and not telling an employee how valuable they are because of the fear they might ask for a raise! Giving up control means we are not totally responsible for the work, and also an unwillingness to share the honors with others.

Sometimes appreciation is overlooked because of the over involvement in the project we are developing to manifestation. While busy keeping the project or desire envisioned and moving in the right direction, the crew can be overlooked. At this level of activity the work can appear to be more like "work" than it was when we were developing our intentions to manifest purpose. Now the work needs more delegating and support to see it through to the end and while being deeply immersed in the maintenance aspects, it is easier to forget who is working and supporting just as much on our behalf. If the crew is getting financial support for their help in supporting our intentions the money acts on behalf of appreciation. *They are getting paid, isn't that enough?* Yet, if the cast and crew are friends and family, it might become, *I would do the same for them*!

I always like to remember that the ones who helped me on the way up will still be there on my way down.

Appreciation is an expression of admiration, approval, or gratitude. It is a benchmark of a leader and extremely valuable in connecting to the real meaning of Abundance.

The difficulty of Self-expression is mirrored in being *reserved*. It is interesting that many reserved individuals are often some of the most *feeling people*. They may feel to the extreme. They feel for people who are the worst off, animals that are abandoned or abused, and world hunger. Yet they are unable to be Self-expressive to the people who are the closest to them.

Oftentimes it is easier for them to give charitably to organizations and yet have little charity at home.

This is found in those individuals referred to as *Type* A behavior people, the type who have a personality that is marked by impatience, aggressiveness, competitiveness and the need to control.

· *I have to do it my way.*
· *It is my way or the highway.*
· *I never can find good employees.*

· *If I don't do it myself, it won't get done.*
· *My way is the only way I know it will work.*
· *Who died and made you king?*
· *It doesn't matter if it is right; it works for me.*
· *You can't teach old dogs new tricks.*
· *It is the only way I know how to do it.*
· *Do you think you can do it any better?*

Delegation is appreciation in the highest form. It says to others, "I will share with you all that I know so far and I am open to receiving all that you have to offer in return."

Delegation is helping others to achieve their goals.

If you do not delegate, it is a form of Self-sabotage which is an act or process tending to hamper or hurt your final outcome. It is an unwillingness to truly accept help from others.

Working Hard for Everything

Those who take the path of least resistance often say the phrase "I do everything easily and effortlessly." It is a phrase that is also the most desired of all sayings in today's world and is the most misused. Why would anyone wish to create anything the easy way? Furthermore, how is it possible in a world that is constructed to be hard to live in? It is a fallible idea that is often placed in the concept of being infallible. Have you ever known anyone who really did anything easily? Whether it is the study of martial arts, yoga or astronomy there is hard work required to master the ideas. If a person is doing something the easy way, it is usually at the expense of someone else picking up the slack!

If anyone is going about anything the easy way, then I doubt much is getting accomplished. I know the easy goers are out there right now contesting this notion, but I say to them, you are over-delegating and under-appreciating those around you who are assisting you on your path.

There is the possibility of creating with grace and ease, but this is created after enduring a great deal of painstaking understanding. It might look easy to everyone else, but the reality is, it came at a price. Everything sweet comes after a great deal of sweat, as the saying goes.

This doesn't mean to suggest that something can't be created with good form and gentleness. The approach is everything. It also doesn't have to *beat you up* in the process either. But everything is supported by gravity and inertia. *Appreciating what it takes to manifest to purpose can reduce the amount of stress involved.* Often there lies the problem of I never thought it would be this hard!

It has everything to do with how we perceive the concept of abundance.

I use to believe I had to work hard for everything I wanted in life. I believed that nothing came easy to me and therefore if I did not go out and get it myself, I would never have it. Now I could have said just as easily that everything comes easily to me and I have it come to me without having to go out and get it for myself.

What I would really be creating is not an easier way to get something, but how I feel about what it is that I am receiving. The work may very well be the same, but my point of view in the value of what I am receiving changes.

It wasn't that I was unwilling to place the necessary energy into an outcome, but how I felt about it was based on struggling to have it created.

The whole abundance concept is being sold by many as simply something that everyone can have easily. This is not true and sounds more like a magic pill. First of all, the concept of abundance is based on the knowing that there is profusion and wealth to be shared, by the Universe and by individuals. *Very few people have prosperity because they shared it.* They have manifested money oftentimes at the expense of others. And as far as the universe is concerned, most people are not even connected to the *knowing* of Higher Self. Where is all this abundance supposed to come from if we do not really feel we are one of the chosen few? I am not here to be the harbinger of news that is not in accordance with what is being presented by the pop culture, but I am here to say that in order to *believe* you are able to have anything you desire, you first have to *know* it. And this is harder than what we have been led to believe. It is much like the idea of the bamboo plant in the "prosperity corner" of a room. It simply isn't enough to stick the plant there and know our prosperity will begin to increase. The entire philosophy of Feng Shui is based on water and air flowing as one; that everything is alive, including the plastic plants in our houses. Everything is *One and the same*. The art of Feng Shui is a way of life, a philosophy of living that insists that all must be in balance in order to create what is desired in the best and highest Good.

Believing the universe is abundant but having little charity at home will not work. Thinking that if the act of concentrating long enough and hard enough on a million dollar bill will fill the bank with unearned income might be an easy sell, but it is much harder to create.

Money, like everything else, is energy that requires direction, intelligence and thought, not to forget a vision that can be held for more than an hour. Abundance is being advertised as prosperity and multi-level marketed by the media. Even the definition of abundance is a *relative* degree of plentifulness. It doesn't mean a cash cow of over-indulgence in the universe! *Relative means having a relation to, or connection with, or necessary dependence on another thing.* It means that believing we can truly have it must first be in alignment with what abundance is in the first place. The place where all possibilities reside in action.

❖ **What does an Abundant Universe mean to you?**

ॐ ॐ ॐ

So let us just say you want a million dollars and think about it all the time and, voila, something happens and you get what you asked for without doing anything in the process. Then what? How hard do you think it will be to keep that money? How much effort and energy do you think you will need to place on this kind of energy to hold onto it? It will take everything you know to understand what the money is teaching you. It will take all the lessons that will be created by how you feel about your Self and everyone in your movie. Will you be able to hold onto the million while you are learning all you need to know to keep it? How many new people will you need to place in your life to help you protect the money? Lawyers, accountants and not to mention, all the relatives and friends who think they have some claim on you and your cash. In your spare time find a millionaire and ask him or her how easy their life is. Manifesting money is hard work; only the appearance of it seems easy.

Manifesting money may be easy. Keeping it is another story.

Regeneration and Unity

The Universal-Mind is indeed here to express for us in all ways; however, it is not here just to give us whatever we ask for in the context of self-indulgence. The Universal-Mind does not concern itself with such offerings because the Human Will can manipulate through an indulgent energetic process and is already more than capable of taking care of such "wants." As co-creators we are able to manifest whatever we require at any given moment. All we need do is put forth the energy and the time, and it can be created. From toothpaste to paper money we have created whatever we have conceived or think we can sell.

The Universal-Mind as abundance has a much bigger plan than we imagine it to have in store for us in our limited beliefs.

In a world which revolves around the notion of self-worth it is hard to imagine there is any other reason to be here except to create more of what it is that we think we want. After all don't most of us live in the land of more?

Self-worth is a relatively new idea. It has only been floating around the planet since the 1940s. It is a young concept, which has taken a real hold on modern mankind. It is what we now compare and contrast all material things to and believe we need to have more of. It is what dreams are made of even in third world nations. It is a post-war concept. After the Second World War the world was in chaos economically and politically. A new industry was emerging and the need to rebuild foreign countries became the new game. Soldiers were coming home and getting married and wanting to start new lives. But there were no jobs in the small towns where they grew up, so the move into larger towns and cities began. The displacement of families and their ties to communities began to unfold. People were moving everywhere in hopes of finding a better life. Communities and towns were no longer cohesive as a large population of young men and women moved to strange, new cities for work.

The value of the towns their parents lived in for the past hundred years was based on the survival of the community. The family doctor, the schoolhouse, the co-op where they shopped and bartered and the churches where they married, christened their young and prayed together in communion were their foundation. Everyone knew each other and there was a sense of belonging. What they did for a living was to help and support the community and they were respected and held in *esteem* for their work. Self-esteem was the benchmark of being respected in the community.

With all the moving and relocating of Americans, the desire to be recognized in the new communities was manufactured by what kind of car you drove and how you dressed. How much money you had became the new benchmark and self-esteem was slowly replaced by the new idea of self-worth. How much of anything owned became the status for respect in the land of more.

Self-worth slowly became the new game of life and everyone wanted to play. Over the years it has become how people judge themselves. So consequently *having* increases self-worth and *losing* lowers self-worth. Having money and things elevates self-worth, but having very little and making very little money lowers self-worth. Prosperity became connected to self-worth and so has the concept of abundance. The limited idea now is the universe has nothing better to do than lavish money on anyone who believes he or she deserves it.

But the universe has a bigger plan. Quite frankly, the universe is not attached to the human drama of money and worth, especially since the feelings by just about everybody are mixed in the first place. Nope, no bankers in outer space eager to send checks in the mail! It is strictly a human desire and oftentimes not one positioned for our Highest Good or in Divine Order.

In the highest vibration of the Divine Self, Abundance is the cycle of Regeneration and Unity.

The Universal Mind, or God within is our Highest Good and is sharing abundance to spiritually renew and revive us, balancing the quality or state of being created as One.

While we are busy living in duplicity, splitting ourselves into a thousand different desires and being multi-faceted selves, the universe is holding the space. Since we do not know that we *already* know because we simply do not believe—in the perfect space we live in, the universe is regenerating and reviving us as we explore our infinite potential and as we journey to purpose. Even while we are living in what we believe is the "Land of More."

The Law of Self-Preservation is in place to remind us that every time we ignore choices along the path to improving ourselves from within we eventually run out of all choices and eventually back ourselves into corners to only act upon the effect of what we have created. We begin to manifest from survival mode. The personal mind will eliminate all possibilities until there are none left and the fear there is a lack of abundance will begin to manifest in believing there is no way out of the situations we have created.

The land of more is not a community. It is a state of personal mind isolated from the world by fear that every material thing we have collected may be taken from us or lost. In the land of more there is never enough.

❖ **What do you create and share in your community?**
❖ **What are you afraid of losing?**
❖ **Give examples of the difference between self-esteem and self-worth.**

Personal Limitations or Spiritual Freedom

The abundance that is discovered in the actions we take with everything we do is produced in large and small ways. It all depends on the personal limitations—the limited beliefs—placed on the results. Limitations are confined in the personal mind but wisdom is the ability to discern inner qualities and relationships to one's Self and to the Universal Mind or God within.

Asking for anything is a degree of limitation.

Asking for anything is suggesting to the sub-conscious mind, the generator which magnifies every thought we focus on, that we do not already have it within ourselves and there is some sort of lack. The suggestion of lack is then magnetized and more lack is manifested. The God Source within already knows what we want and it is the personal mind that is only unconscious of it.

The Conscious/Unconscious Mind is limited by the degree of understanding we have of who we *think* we are and what we are able to create based on personal limited beliefs connected to how the Dangerous/Beautiful Mind identifies our role in our movies.

Words like impossible, or "it can never happen," are easily thought because of negative affirmed programs associated with past stories we have made up in our journey. The idea that "everything is possible" may only apply to future events or a possible future world and so intentions necessary to create realities are not held by vision. An example is the idea of world peace or interplanetary space travel. These intentions are relegated to dreams, however in the imagination they already exist.

The speed at which anyone could run a foot race remained the same speed for decades until the next person in history ran a race much faster than anyone had ever run before. Once this was accomplished others began to run as fast. The Dangerous Mind will say it cannot be done and so it becomes "truth" for the collective. Yet a foot runner imagined he could run faster than anyone before him and held the vision in his mind's eye. Through positive affirmed thought he *intended* to break the previous speed record.

Once one singular creative thought within us observes it is possible to hold an intention that it can do something that has never been done before, the opportunity for a quantum leap begins to take place.

People who the world have often called mad think impossible dreams. Once the impossible becomes accomplished those same people are called innovative geniuses.

We are what stars are made of, so is it possible that we shine as bright, illuminating the personal and infinite space we embody.

Light is said to have the appearance of darkness in space. The cosmic Light we are a part of does not reflect upon itself because it simply is All There Is. It has nothing to reflect upon and, therefore, cannot be seen.

The personal limitations of the Dangerous Mind cannot see the Light. So the Dangerous Mind does not comprehend it.

The goals the Conscious Self creates are, most of the time, within the limitations of the total collective consciousness of humanity and a person searches no further.

I get what I ask for in small ways every day; I just don't easily see it.

What is honored in the asking only becomes visible when it is appreciated. The asking need not be *consciously understood to be known*, but it does require the gratitude manifested in appreciation.

Every small desire is our Highest Self, endowed with motion.

Whether we believe it or not, every moment we are creating something new in our personal universe, and it is only a microcosm of the greater Universal Mind living inside each of us. The Universal Mind inside is the Bigger Picture, making a difference every time we stretch personal limitations, our limited beliefs, by helping others with gentle nudges and guidance.

We are all gently nudging and guiding each other. We are herding energy into a myriad of directions every day, pushing the collective consciousness closer to the cliff of imagined dreams. We jump off the cliff, and then we build our wings on the way down. Within each of us is the unconscious/conscious desire to grow and progress into the wholeness of perfect Self. And without knowing that we know, we are nudging, helping others to achieve their goals and in return we gain *spiritual fulfillment in a concrete world.*

Discovery

1. Why did you choose to come to Planet Earth? Imagine for a moment.

2. What would you do today if this were the last day you were here on Earth?

3. What catastrophic events are taking place right now on Earth? What do these events mirror to us about ourselves?

4. Life is hard until you figure out that it actually is difficult and then decide to make it as easy on your Self as you can. In what ways can you create an easier life?

5. What does an Abundant Universe mean to you?

6. What do you create and share in your community?

7. What are you afraid of losing?

8. Give examples of the differences between self-esteem and self-worth.

9. We are biologically connected to each other. We are chemically connected to the Earth. We are atomically connected to the Universe. What does this mean to you?

10. How do you value yourself?

11. Sit down and email your groups, friends and family and ask

them to describe in a few words how they value you. Ask them to express what gifts and talents you offer and give to them.

Everyday Affirmations

I am whole.

Every time I feel lack I remember to appreciate what I have created.

I am connected to everything.

I am open and willing to receive all that is given with kindness and love.

I am a child of the Universe.

I am in this moment, on this day happy with who I am.

Everything is as it should be in my world.

I remember to bless every living thing everyday.

I appreciate my journey.

Where am I? Who am I?
How did I come to be here?
What is this thing called the world?
How did I come into the world?
Why was I not consulted?
And If I am compelled to take part in it,
Where is the director?
I want to see him.

- Soren Kierkegaard

Chapter 9

Integrity

Leadership by Example

An important quality of being a great leader is the ability to guide by example through honesty that is undivided. It comes from expressing the heart's wisdom and Higher Consciousness of the God-Self and not the mental or logical state of the personal mind connecting to the Spiritual Laws journeyed from consequences of unconscious reactions. It is why we are growing through the journey of life discovering the value of being true to one's Self. We are guided and progressively propelled to the fulfillment of life's purpose.

Abundance is the *regeneration* of the Spiritual Self and holds the space of unity in the revelation that *we are all One* reflected in the infinite experience of Spirit. Abundance guides by example and supports humanity's *redemption* to manifest *love as the power* on our journey known as *The Way*.

The way of love is the art of inner wisdom. It is discovered from living the teachings abundance expresses in its example that there is only cosmic freedom, which is not found in the outer journey in the "land of more" but in the inner Universal Mind of the Soul/ Spirit unified field of consciousness. The outer journey is here to reflect and mirror to us the *inner* way in which we are evolving and expressing. We are the *excellent journey* and the power of love is perfect in the expression of the Self.

Abundance is having the Wisdom in knowing there is no thing to lose.

Leadership by example in its Highest Good is through integrity. The Authentic Self is honest and knows *I am the role model*. Our journey is to remember Who I Am in the Highest Self.

The fear of realizing we are the role models dwells in the Dangerous Mind insisting that living "above the radar" will only bring repeated consequences of pain and sorrow. And the Dangerous Mind, the negative affirmed thoughts, believes this to be the path of the Martyr. This belief is held by the Dangerous Mind because of the fear that the greatest sacrifice and death will be the personal mind for another state of greater value. The Dangerous Mind fears it will be sacrificed and will do everything in its power to prevent us from making this decision through a consciously aware choice!

I AM the role model.

The integrity realized in being the role model is blazing a trail of initiation for all those who desire to know the Self and the Abundant Wisdom of the heart's desire to remove sorrow. *The Way*, or the movie-making journey of *My Life*, is here on this planet to realize our Highest Good and to improve conditions for humanity.

No one gets left behind.

Leadership is guiding by example and can be a cause for viewing and observing the good or bad in all us. It is what makes us fearful of being ready, able and, most importantly, willing to lead by example.

· *What if I mess it up?*
· *What if I do a horrible job and cause others or myself to suffer?*
· *Who am I to lead anybody?*

Being open to step into the Light of leadership is to be honest enough to know mistakes are the constant gifts of Self-examining awareness. Making mistakes to further improve, rewrite and revise the script of the human experience manifests honesty and integrity. We are leading by example every day whether we are aware of this or not. Becoming aware of how we are leading by example is the personal journey of the Self, explored by the higher example of the Universal God-Mind within.

Do I lead by example for the Best and Highest Good?

Ambition

The desire to achieve a particular end is to aspire to something higher than oneself and usually implies that the striver is thereby ennobled. Being ennobled is to be elevated, not just in one aspect but integrated in Abundant Spirit, Universal Mind and Manifested Body. The true achievement is the awareness that all the illusions of the fragmented Self are One and balanced. Like a "mirror ball" the aware Self reflects all those we encounter on the journey.

What does this mean? It means that as we vibrate at a higher frequency we will attract equally elevated vibrations of everything around us.

When I am enlightened, so are the trees and the stars.

If we are involved in an environment of lower vibrational frequency, the more aware we become of the One Self, the higher the vibration raises around us! We become guides to all who desire to raise their vibrations, simply because we are participating in our own personal awareness with a desire to be elevated. Like attracts like. It is a beautiful thing and perfect. We are the role models whether we know it or not. Becoming attuned to higher vibrations results in every lower vibration surrounding us to resonate to the higher vibration we emit. It sounds quantum, and it is!

But why is it that oftentimes the surrounding environment seems to bring us down instead of raising to the new frequency?

Remember the question *What is Love?*

What was discovered is love flows at the highest vibration, but what is attached to love is how the vibration is lowered and weighted down. The more something is attached to love, the lower the understanding of *What love is not*! manifests. This applies to all aspects of any vibration. Depending on how much of an emotional attachment we place on any vibration, the lower the outcome. If we are feeling good about who we are in our make believe movie today, yet attaching to how others feel, we will begin to feel as they feel. It is the attachment to others' feelings which will filter Divine Love reducing the vibrational feelings. The momentary "high" once felt has gone because of attaching emotionally to what is happening around us.

Whether it is the need for others to know how we feel or our need to help them instead of *guiding* by example, it is still the attachment of *need*. Guiding turns to an ambition to help. Once there is any attachment for any reason, our vibration, no matter how high the achievement, turns to an ambition to be more involved emotionally in someone else's journey, their movie, and the burden of attachment lowers all of our vibrations to align with the surrounding environment. We magnetize core issues over and over again until we recognize what the core issues are attempting to reveal. "Clearing" negative affirmed thoughts, in the personal mind, is only removing them superficially.

The core *issues*, or the internal memory of the subconscious will continue to magnetize further negativity. When we become more aware of what it is we are attracting, not by asking the "why?" but instead through the observer's eye as the "what?" we can begin looking within to the subconscious negative programs to discover core issues connected to past stories we are still holding in the mind. Without the deeper journey within Self, whatever continues to be attracted as "lack" (to "self hatred"), will be gifted to us by the outer world we are attracting.

Remember, mistakes are simply changes in growth of consciousness to awareness. Do not take anything personally when it is self-attracted, instead recognize the Gift and look inward to what is magnetizing it in the first place.

Ambition can become an attachment to striving for a goal.

The desire to achieve a particular end can be perceived as either attractive or discouraging to those around us. The need to take others (family, friends, associates) along interferes with our ability to hold the highest intentions, and the *need* to have others understand what we are doing or who we are becoming is the distraction. Once distracted the Gift is mirrored in the attachment. Many times even ambition becomes the distraction on any journey.

The need to fix anyone, including your Self, is a distraction from Higher Purpose.

For one hundred years we have lived in a world of *future* ambitions coupled with self-determination to have it all now. In the last fifty years we have seen the rise of the "super-achievers." Societies in general are determined to accomplish as much, in the land of more, as they can achieve. The need to accomplish and acquire as much of everything as possible has led to an even greater desire for more balance with *what for*? The need to accomplish has led to the desire to tear down the old and to preserving it anew—the desire to hoard and then to share, or to keep or give away. Ambition for Higher Self has become the motto for the New Age achievers. Sometimes the ambition is mirrored in the awareness of *idealism*, a theory that the essential nature of reality lies in consciousness or reason. However, the coupling is only now becoming manifested in what is really the New Age—the knowing that whatever we create as individuals ultimately we are responsible for nurturing and for being accountable for at the outcome.

Human Beings are the problem-solvers of the New Age.

It is what we do best and worst. It is what sets us apart from the rest of the animal kingdom. We create everything to observe it. We create to complete and to begin again with fresher eyes. It is what we think we do best. We create problems so we can solve them. Sometimes we take the entire problem and cut it up into little confounded pieces to puzzle it back together again. We do this with our lives, the planet and maybe even as a ripple effect in the physical universe.

We disseminate so we can unify.

We sow the seeds of Who I Am to reflect Who We Are to know Who I Am. This is the true nature of humanity as *beings of progress*. But the ambition to *believe* before we *know* and *achieve* before we *become* disconnects us from knowing who I really AM.

§ § §

You are the Role Model.

You are out on the leading edge of Creation eagerly creating! And in striving to solve all that you create you become attached to the process of becoming, forgetting that all you are required to do is Be Who You Are.

§ § §

We are solving everything at the exact same rate we are becoming aware.

Responsibility

Ambition and idealism are culminated in completion of the intention. The intention is held from an active vision of what we desire. Whether it is something the mind is in pursuit of attaining, by manifesting thoughts into reality, or from the heart's desire to remember love, the instructions and teachings are journeyed because of a desire for realization as completion.

The Higher Self knows we are accountable for everything we create.

So why is it so hard to admit responsibility for what we are doing? Perhaps because accountability has been relegated to religions that tell us that God will save us or the State, which only wants to control us will save us, responsibility has been relegated to a few who govern the many or the god(s) that governs us all. Whichever it may be, we are taught from a very early age that we only have a small part to play and we need to be managed. Religions generally have some golden parachute attached, like heaven, or are grouped together conveniently to create an easy exit.

In Japan many people during their life follow the Shinto Religion with their deities and god emperor but closer to death they convert to Buddhism. The Catholic Religion uses popes and priests as go-betweens to ask for absolution of their followers. But in all of the major beliefs held, there is always some God form outside of the human experience that is in control and sees the bigger picture.

The biggest picture is the one inside each of us and we are responsible for all of it.

How can I be responsible for everything? Because we are One. We are the only One. Whatever else we are, we are the only God there Is. And the only One that is holding us accountable is our Self.

Taking responsibility for our Self is the big picture. And once we are aware of this we are elevated to the God-Mind within. The "ascension" process is *internal* not external. No god(s), alien "mother ships," religions or governments are going to rescue us. Wake up! The dream or belief in the rescue is the real enemy of us all and as long as we collectively hold this vision, we will continue to be slaves. It continues to perpetuate the idea that we are not solely responsible for our actions. All shifts of consciousness to a higher degree of awareness are the ways to elevating beyond the field of problems, which cannot be fixed or solved, to a higher consciousness above the field of problems.

To be free all we are required to do is to stand up and be free.

Whether we believe in life after death or not, the physical universe reminds us that for every season there is a turn, a change. As long as we believe that we are never returning to this field of problems in the birth-death-reincarnation cycle, we will continue to believe the responsibility for the ultimate effects of our actions is not our own. However, as long as we act within the field of problems we are trapped in unconsciousness. We are growing whether we believe it or not and we are affecting the physical universe in turn.

This is our wake up call to become citizens of the God-Mind within and enjoy all the movies we are making up. We can only enjoy this cinematic adventure when experienced in the Best and Highest Good for ALL. Not a few and not the many but all of us.

Idealism

Did you know that idealism is only a theory? It is a theory that ultimate reality lies in a realm transcending phenomena and that the essential nature of reality lies in consciousness or reason. And why shouldn't it be? Since all that most people believe to be true is only perceived through the five senses, even the Mind, whether Dangerous or Beautiful, is believed to be only the chemical *goo* manufactured by the brain.

There is only the One and the individual thoughts that separate us from it. We are the thoughts in the Universal Mind, or God within.

And the Universe is a holographic image of what is inside the Self.

But this to is only a theory yet to be understood.

The theory of idealism remains a theory for the time being because the understanding and the reality of it have yet to be experienced in our collective human consciousness. Idealism is only an idea, a concept of what may be found to be actual, or real in some future place and time, perhaps a future "here" or on some other distant planet. Yet there are billions of people living here on this planet holding this theory to be possible. They hold a vision collectively that affirms the preeminent value of imagination as compared with faithful copying of nature. *Imagination* is the act or power of forming a mental image of something not present to the senses or never before wholly perceived in reality.

Imagine.

The Humanitarian Conscious Self

Connecting the dots.
In the beginning there is:

1. The Seed of Intention.
2. Nurtured by Intuition.
3. Clarified in Creativity.
4. Solidified through Commitment.
5. Strengthened in Trust.
6. Developed in Application.
7. Understood in "the Work."
8. Supported in Abundant Wisdom.
9. Manifested to Purpose.

The journey comes full circle in finally knowing either achievement or failure. Whatever the endgame is, it is what we have created, and if we are consciously aware, we know the ultimate responsibility is ours and ours alone.

Or is it?

Does anyone ever do anything alone? Is the decision-making made from just our Self? Was everything based on just our original thoughts? Of course not! So why would we have the full responsibility of the outcome? Because we would have it no other way. Because no matter how many suggestions, expert helpers, cast and crew that helped manifest it, we held the original vision from Source and made the choices, good or bad, right or wrong that held it together until it was completed. In the end, we are the One who was there from the beginning to the endgame. The alpha and the omega. Each of us held the big picture in the thoughts compelled outward from Source and then made it into a thousand little puzzle pieces just to put it all back together again. The One creative thought propelled forward, growing exponentially into infinite possibility. We may have had help at times with getting the puzzle put back together, but we are the ones who started it and the ones who finished it. Whether it is a small daily intention or the biggest one in each lifetime lived, we have the biggest picture of how it all came to happen and how it all is to be completed. Whether it is for the Best and Highest good or against our better judgment, it is ours to formulate to purpose. It changes our life in both small ways and in the biggest ways. It is our stories to tell. It is our stories to share. It is our stories to know from what we have communicated and expressed. And then from imitating all that we have been guided to be, we then are able to guide and lead by example.

I have listened to many people's *My Life Movie, Part (place a number for whatever life they are presently living)* and I have never heard the same story. What I have become aware of is how much I respect other people's processes or paths. I listen and oftentimes say *"Wow!"* In turn, they look at me and smile and say how it has not been anything special, nothing worth writing about. *Nothing worth writing about?* Whatever a person has done, and no matter how incredible that person's life has been, most people think that their lives have been "normal" or the same as everybody else's. Not true. Our lives are magnificent and wondrous and *ours!* What this means is we have taken everybody else's historical experiences and have begun to imitate them only to ultimately create something that only each one of us can create through the God-Self, or Highest Consciousness. No one can ever create anyone else's life and we create each of our own from the Source within.

No one can ever create what you have created. You are a unique thought in the Universal Mind.

Now all that is required is to take complete and total responsibility for how excellent your life is. Take ownership of your movie!

Throughout the chapters we have followed the concept of how important it is to take every step and thoroughly pay attention to what is required for completing each vibration from <u>intention</u> to <u>trust</u> and completion of <u>purpose</u>. What is ignored, hurried through, and impatiently passed over are most often the very details we require to be fully understood. Connecting with what we *least enjoy doing* while we are making our movie called *My Life*, are the important spiritual tools to develop, through time and practice, to realize each *purpose unfolding*. The resistances to each step along "the way," the tapping into the Gifts of reflective learning in the process of doing, are the requirements for developing life step-by-step. As said, the very things <u>least developed and understood</u> become the lessons, and sometimes the hardships that are processed over and over again until the Human Will finally surrenders and releases the *need* to control from the "I can't" or "I don't like" negative affirmed thought programs.

There is a reason for learning each step of the journey and knowing that all will be created for the Best and Highest Good. It is the vibration required to mirror back at our Self for the *greatest and highest good within Humanity*. It is our individual contributions as co-creators and collaborators in collective communal reality. It is the mirror of *namaste*, or the God in me sees the God in you. Better yet, the God in me is the God in you!

It is when we understand the purpose of all we manifest and then translate the idealistic into the practical that we become the positive affirmed cultural leaders, the cultural guides to be imitated, and then uniquely individualized in Self-expression, that we may share with others in true joy.

The humanitarian places people before things.

The true humanitarian, who surfaces from the Authentic Self and actualizes into the Transparent Self, works from the quiet Wisdom of the Heart. Not just the "heart" as feeling but the center of the Universe-Mind as the Transparent Heart that requires no reflection, knowing that all is One and no longer requires a mirror to reflect itself.

The cultural humanitarian is elevated into the Higher Vibration of Love because the lessons are no longer repeated for one's Self. The steps from Intention to Purpose are effortlessly followed with Joy, no longer creating obstacles to remind us that <u>we are required to do all the steps</u>. We are creating *everything to purpose* in order to guide by example.

The humanitarian reflects the inherent Wisdom versus the Lessons of Life.

As the role model we realize the only movie we desire to create is our own aspect of Universal Mind. And that *being* is a higher vibration than doing. Through conscious awareness we understand attaching <u>to anything or anyone</u> lowers the vibration of the Self and connects us either to the Dangerous Mind or to the Beautiful Mind, thereby no longer allowing to be directed effortlessly by the deeper Guide of the Heart of the God-Mind within.

The humanitarian knows the Highest Spiritual Wisdom cannot be found in the mind alone.

Discovery

1. Examine the skills you have manifested in your life which express leadership qualities. Make a list and appreciate what you already have learned.

2. In what ways are you a role model in your community? Family? Friends? Ask people how they view you personally, professionally and spiritually.

3. With all the money, time and opportunity in the world what will you create of value for the human race as a humanitarian?

4. In making the movie called "My Life" ask yourself, "Who is directing my movie?" Someone else? You? God?

5. What part of you believes there will be a rescue mission from outside yourself? How much responsibility are you willing to take for the movie called "My Life?"

6. Write a new script of your life from this moment forward. Add everything you wish for your Self to experience on this journey.

7. Write a short memoir of your life from old age. What are the highlights of your life?

Everyday Affirmations

I am a role model.
I am the beginning and the end and the beginning again.

I am ready, able and willing to be free.

I am discovering and exploring each day with fresh eyes.

I am open and receiving for my best and highest good everyday.

I am healthy, prospered and fulfilled from the Source of who I am.

I am meditating daily.

I am Love and everything else is an illusion.

I love my Self as the God Mind within is Love.

I am no longer asleep.

I am awake!

Thought Glossary

From the beginning of the Journey, starting with the Intention, whatever we create is for our best and highest good and will be created in Divine Order. We are allowed to create everything the Abundant Universe gifts. We are the receiver of Perfect Love as much as the giver that empowers the Universe in return.

We are the Journey we create, or as the movie, we make manifest in whatever we desire once acceptance and allowance of the Spiritual Laws are placed into action.

The journey of Life is discovering with Love the map of manifestation. Life purpose is to awaken everyday and in every moment experiencing as much as we allow ourselves to receive. It is to practice the width and deepen the breadth in knowing the Spiritual Laws to continue to co-create with deeper states of personal awareness! Let us all enjoy the Journey!

ﬗ ﬗ ﬗ

Abundance

We are provided with all we need, with all we could ever want, in any lifetime. The Universe distributes equally with ever flowing presence, a kaleidoscope of infinite possibility without limitations or interests. We ask and receive at the exact proportion we allow. The Universe is an offering ever flowing never "wanting." When we look to nature in its constant regeneration and unity, we see this also in our Self. At anytime when we do not know the Universe is abundant, we can take a peek at how much we appreciate what we have, know, love, give and receive in our journey of life. At anytime we can make a list of all that we require (or believe we require) and then match the list with everyone we know. We see that all is available to us

273

in the asking, helping and sharing of lives. If we are miserly with ourselves to our Self then it is simply a matter of opening not only the receivership but to begin to *allow* ourselves to receive. We love outside our Self at the exact same frequency we love inside our Self. All the abundance we so much wish for others can be found first in loving our Self. Appreciate our Self for who we imagine ourselves to be when we understand that we are already fully aware but just do not know it yet!

೫ ೫ ೫

Balance

The ebb and flow of all life begins with breathing. Look to the natural process to reflect in our Self what nature already does. Whenever we are breathing in a shallow manner, the Will center of the chest is blocking the passageway between the mind and the heart and will constrict the flow of energy in the physical body creating a sense of restraint. Remembering to balance happens naturally as energy flows in—energy flows out. Being still and being aware of the nature of breathing will bring balance in our lives. Imbalance happens when any form (thought/idea, action/work) becomes extreme and fatigued. Life is managing itself in perfect awareness of itself. In the human experience we can have choice in conscious awareness and we can make the choice to choose being imbalanced. Often times we perceive balance as only two sided, like a seesaw, or polarity. The Universe is multi-dimensional, multi-faceted and multi-sided maintaining everything in the balance as the One.

ჰ ჰ ჰ

Cause and Effect

From Spirit all is creation in the material world and Spirit is not created because it is not material. Spirit is the cause and all that we observe is the effect. *Does Spirit imagine?* I say "yes," because we imagine and manifest from no-thing to some-thing everyday. We only must become aware of who is creating all that we imagine knowing that we are the maker of our thoughts—not our thoughts created. There is a point in the human experience when the knowing through awareness is that we are One and the same. At once we are able to create all we imagine and all we are also co-creating with every other thing. Together we are responsible for what we do and equally responsible for what every other thing does. The material Universe is a collaboration of all things from Spirit. A God/Spirit manifest in Man/Woman/Material is One however, as Man/Woman/Material we *think* we are separate manifesting ideas which create cause and effect. No thing is created/manifested without a creator. Living in the material, men and women resound to all creation and may at times judge what has been created by God as perfect and yet not see himself or herself as perfect. Men/Women will then judge all that they create as imperfect in return. In our human experience we are blessing our Self with the gift of all that we reflect in all that we attract. Once we understand through awareness what we see is only a reflection of Who We Are, then we can change. I often say truth is liquid, flowing like the Universe. Like a river, it is always present yet never remains in the same place.

၅ ၅ ၅
Communication

Everything in the Universe is communicating; both through the Universal Mind as Spirit and through the material Universe. Vibrations are being exchanged back and forth through frequencies as everything, or All There Is. Communication is simply a signal that is being sent by one field to and received by another. If both fields are in alignment the signal is understood. In our smaller universe of the physical experience here on Earth, we are sending and receiving signals both verbal and non-verbal, all the time. We are also sending and receiving on the physical and non-physical levels of our Universe.

The field that we are aspiring to understand the most effectively is the field we call Love. Whatever the signal is called by any other name—joy, bliss, happiness, ecstasy, or peace—it is the true nature of the human experience to remember. Suspended in the theory of gravity and magnetism is the tiny speck called "me", here on this blue planet, in this solar system, on the outer edge of this galaxy which is spiraling and spinning in a Universe expanding with our family of billions (if not trillions) of other such galaxies, millions of light years wide and clustered together in chains of fluid rivers of energy. In this tiny place inside our body is a sensitive array signaling to everything in the Universe. We are beacons tapping into the signal of Spirit and whether we are allowing it or not the signal is always Love. It is what we all share in common in this unified field of consciousness. We are communicating all the time, everyday and in every moment to each other and to our Self. What we hear from everything is "all is well in the Universe." What we are beginning to understand is that we are sharing the same communication with each other in our human attempt to transmute all that we do not understand into Love.

§ § §
# Compensation

Compensation is a blueprint whereby we cover-up—consciously or unconsciously— weaknesses, frustrations, desires, feelings of inadequacy or incompetence in our life areas through the gratification or (drive towards) excellence in other areas. Compensation can cover-up imagined lack and personal or physical feelings of believing we are less than everyone else. The compensation strategy however, does not truly address the source of feeling lack. Positive compensations may help one to overcome difficulties. On the other hand, negative compensations do not, which results in reinforced feelings of lack. There are two kinds of negative compensation:

Overcompensation, characterized by a superiority goal, leads to striving for power, dominance, self-esteem and self-devaluation.

Undercompensation, which includes a demand for help, leads to a lack of courage and a fear for life.

Often times the requirement for compensation is cleared when we no longer do what we believe is the right or wrong thing, but achieve balance through becoming the role model by doing what we love and being authentic with Who We Are on the inside.

Shame and guilt are connected to believing we are not whole and that there is some innate flaw inside ourselves that will forever prevent us from being free from judgement. Remember, judgement is only an opinion held by ourselves and others. I often state that our opinion of ourselves is none of our business or anyone else's. More importantly, their opinion of us is equally of no concern to the truth of who we really are inside. Judging ourselves is equal to the amount we judge others, including Life itself!

§ § §
# Retribution

When any thought, deed or feeling is created with the belief that there will be some kind of recompense (either a reward or a punishment), this is known as retribution. The old saying, "You reap what you sow," should only be about farming but unfortunately it has the "eye for an eye" agenda connected to it. This is archaic thinking by the way. It is a life created to believe that there is some sort of payback involved. No wonder so many believe the Universe should just write them a check! Breathing becomes services rendered and should be compensated when actually the concept is more connected to our good and bad actions, or deeds. As long as the human experience is based on ideas of "good" being rewarded, and if we create a crime, or "bad," we will be punished—we will continue to give power and focus to both the need for tribute (a payment one to another in acknowledgment of submission or as the price of protection)—by those who enslave thoughts and deeds, and to that which is believed to be governing in the hereafter.

There is no benefit in claiming judgment over who have been "naughty or nice." Collectively we have determined that wherever a person is born, he is responsible for upholding the laws that govern the community. That, of course, is only viable as long as everyone agrees the community is in alignment with everyone else's community and this is un-claimable (as in asserting the possibility of contradictions).

We live on a planet broken up into communities that contradict each other to such an extent the mirror of life is in the gift that no one set of enforced laws appears to work for everyone. Creating anything with the thoughts of getting something in return and any motivation with an agenda which causes harm to another living thing, will continue to nurture the belief and value of retribution as another form of slavery.

§ § §

Sequence

Life, like a movie, is a succession of related shots or scenes developing a single subject or phase of a film story. Life on Earth is only one of a million possible stories we are creating. Life is a sequence, an episode that is played out in unison with everyone else. It seems large and most of the time small compared to the bigger picture. But we are assured—it is what is required in the grand order of things. Without every grain of sand there can be no beach for the waves to ebb and flow. In an infinite singularity every possibility exists and connects sequentially to the whole. Like DNA and the exact order of nucleic acids or amino acids are the foundation for life itself, there is a sequence occurring. There is an exact order to everything and even chaos has order!

The journey through life can be observed as a sequence of events and each event preceding the next will determine the probable outcome of each event. No two events are alike, so most likely each event *wills* all future events. It does not appear that life is some pre-determined story that we are simply playing out while we are in the human experience. More likely, as our awareness expands, so do the probable outcomes of each event in our story. The amount of awareness we receive and allow to come into our lives will be proportionate to how vast the expansion of consciousness will be.

Let's observe life in the same way Leonardo Pisano might have observed it. He asked the question in the thirteenth century, "How many pairs of rabbits will be produced in a year, beginning with a single pair, if in every month each pair bears a new pair which becomes productive from the second month on?" Known as The *Fibonacci Sequence* the question became a fascination to people for centuries mainly because the answer explored the aesthetics found in nature. The answer, in rabbits no less, showed the first pair again in the second month (keeping in mind the original pair produced in the first month is not yet mature), and in the third month 2 pairs will be produced, one by the original pair and one by the pair which was produced in the first month. So by the fourth month 3 pairs will be produced, and in the fifth month 5 pairs. After these smaller pairs things expand rapidly, and we get the following sequence of numbers:

1, 1, 2, 3, 5, 8, 13, 21, 34, 55, 89, 144, 233....

The amazing result of this phenomenon is the aesthetic beauty observed for all to see. Masters of the transcendental refer to it as "progress." The word *progress* by the enlightened is not the same sort of progress we associate with in smaller terms. It perhaps refers to the idea of the enfolding and unfolding of everything in the Universe not merely the idea of "gradual betterment." When we look at the numbers in the Fibonacci Sequence starting from the smallest number in the center spiraling outward, it is observed that the size and proportions expand fairly equally to size of the numbers. Using a selection of boxes to illustrate outward spiraling effect it then looks something like this.

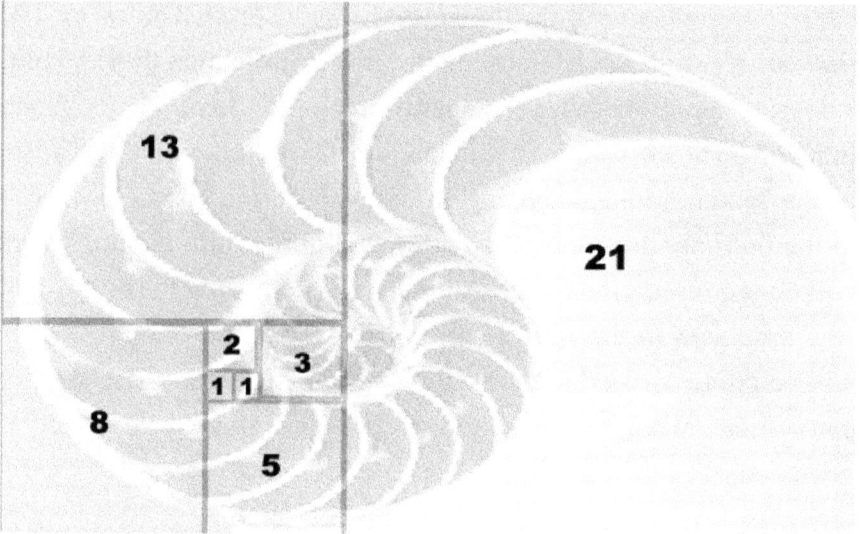

This spiraling effect is found repeatedly in nature and is beauti-fully represented in the journey of galaxies. In Chapter One the number one is symbolic of the Hero on the heroic journey. The Hero—all of us—from birth represents the seed of all things possible to become manifest. The infinite singularity grows and expands through a sequence of events into greater and greater awareness. In the Hero's being, (and remember the *Hu* in human means God), is the God-ness exploring Is-ness of Man expanding and exploring the Universe.

ⓢ ⓢ ⓢ
Continuity

The uninterrupted connection, succession, or union is the basis for any form in continuity. How we experience continuity in our lives is from the connections i.e. relationships, career/money/success, and in the form of scenarios and scripts. Taking a look at the reflection of our past scenarios, it is easier to observe the uninterrupted connection to life's adventure. It does not seem so easy to look at the future in the same way. The unknown can often times leave a person feeling queasy inside. Somehow it is perceived that whatever the future has in store will somehow be different than is anticipated. But why should it be? Taking a peek into our past, we can easily examine where we have been and know how it was interconnected or entwined through the sequence of events called *My Life*. So why does it feel so complex to do the same with our present future?

Reflecting on where we have been will explain the events (both causes and effects) of how we arrived here in the present, and when we re-examine we will see continuity and flow in progress. Everything we have created up to this very moment is unfolding in the grand scheme of our lives. How we feel today is based on what we have experienced. Of course, many people believe that in an instance we can change our thoughts and somehow this will immediately affect our future. Perhaps a better course of action will be to know that what we think is based on how we feel; not the other way around. How we feel projects what thoughts we will attach and which of the thousands of thoughts that bubble up in our heads everyday we will focus our attention on. Why do we pick the thoughts we think? Most of the time it is out of habit. How we feel about who and what we are doing, thinking and saying reinforces the habits, or programs we are utilizing.

If we are really honest with ourselves, we can examine a typical day in life—today—and discover in this moment there is a certain same-ness. There is an underlayment to all that we do and think—to all thinking and action. And perhaps there is a correspondence between the two that can only be understood by becoming aware of how we really feel about life and the lives of each other.

In tapping into the uninterrupted connections, the successions (sequences), or unions, (coalition of humanity) we observe the waves crashing on the beach, one after another with an ongoing rhythm, which appears to have no separation between one wave and another. We have flowed onto Earth from a seed, an infinite singularity which observed in the Fibonacci Sequence is a spiraling Universe within the Universal Mind, continuing to express itself into a form estimated at over 6.6 billion people and counting and not including all other life forms on this blue ball.

卐 卐 卐

Correspondence

We become the architect of ourselves when we become the architect of our minds. The Law of Correspondence, the agreement of things with one another, is a mystical law dating back over three thousand years and presented in both the Vedas and the teaching of Hermes Tristmegistus, a legendary author of works. In these teachings which have been translated throughout history in many forms, we have revised the mystery of life with an understanding that whatever is above us is below us. The outer world in which we live is created from the inner world first. In terms pertaining to the human body, we can also suggest that the mind (what is above) is directly connected to the body (what is below). Whatever we create in the mind is manifested in the body. Knowing this we can realize that which the mind first thinks is seen in the body. The Universe is filled with planets in motion, yet we do not know how they are able to move for we are not able to discover the mind of these objects or what directs them, and yet they exist. In our minds we do not see the thoughts we think but the action of the thoughts when manifested. We may cut a finger and the nervous system will send a message to the brain which will in return send whatever is required to heal the cut in the body. We do not see the thoughts but only the action of the thoughts in the healing process. When we are mentally unhealthy and uneasy, the body will mirror the thoughts as illness and dis-ease. So as we are able to change our thoughts we can change the outcome in the correspondence of our bodies. In the human body everything is mind the same way everything in the Universe is Universal Mind. Wherever we look, there we are. Our greatest responsibility in our lives is to create within ourselves the life we want to create.

References and Reading List

Chapter One

Capra, Fritjof. *The Tao of Physics: An Exploration of the Parallels between Modern Physics and Eastern Mysticism.* New York: Random House, 2000.

Dyer, Wayne W. *The Power of Intention: Learning to Co-Create You World Your Way.* Carlsbad, CA: Hay House, 2005.

Goldsmith, Joel S. *The Art of Meditation.* New York: HarperCollins Publishers, 1990.

Hicks, Esther. *The Amazing Power of Deliberate Intent: Living the Art of Allowing.* Carlsbad, CA: Hay House, 2005.

Maltz, Maxwell. *Psycho-Cybernetics: A New Way to Get More Living out of Life.* New York: Simon &Schuster Adult Publishing Group, 1976.

Zukav, Gary. *The Dancing Wu Li Masters: An Overview of the New Physics.* New York: HarperCollins Publishers, 2001.

Chapter Two

Baron-Reid, Colette. *Messages from Spirit: The Extraordinary Power of Oracles, Omen, and Signs.* Carlsbad, CA: Hay House, 2008.

--- *Remembering The Future: The Path to Recovering Intuition.* Carlsbad, CA: Hay House, 2006.

Choquette, Sonia. *Trust Your Vibes.* Carlsbad, CA: Hay House, 2004.

Eagle, White. *White Eagle on Intuition and Initiation.* Hants, UK: White Eagle Publishing Trust, 2006.

Holland, John. *Power of the Soul: Inside Wisdom for an Outside World.*

Carlsbad, CA: Hay House, 2008.

--- Psychic Navigator: *Empowering Your Inner Guidance*. Carlsbad, CA: Hay House, 2004.

Millman, Dan. *The Life You Were Born to Live: A Guide to Finding Your Life Purpose*. Tiburon, CA: Starseed Press, 1995.

Phillips, David A. *The Complete Book of Numerology: Discovering the Inner Self*. Carlsbad, CA: Hay House, 2005.

Roman, Sanaya. *Opening To Channel: How to Connect with Your Guide*. Tiburon, CA: Starseed Press, 1993.

--- *Personal Power Through Awareness: A Guidebook for Sensitive People, Vol. 2*. Tiburon, CA: Starseed Press, 1986.

Virtue, Doreen. *Angel Therapy Meditations*. (Compact Disc.) Carlsbad, CA: Hay House, 2008.

--- *How to Hear Your Angels*. Carlsbad, CA: Hay House, 2007.

Reiki Books

Rand, William Lee. *Reiki, the Healing Touch: First and Second Degree Manual, Vol.*, Southfield, MI: Vision Publications - Reiki Webstore, 2000.

Stein, Diane. *Essential Reiki Teaching Manual: An Instructional Guide for Reiki Healers*. Berkeley, CA: The Crossing Press, 2007.

Chapter Three

Cameron, Julia. *The Artist's Way: A Spiritual Path to Higher Creativity*. New York: Penguin Group, 2002.

Fritz, Robert. *The Path of Least Resistance: Learning to Become the Creative Force in Your Own Life.* New York: Random House Publishing Group, 1989.

Goldberg, Natalie. *Writing Down the Bones.* Boston: Shambhala Publication, 1986.

Virtue, Doreen. *Angel Medicine: How to Heal the Body and Mind with the Help of the Angels.* Compact Disc. Carlsbad, CA: Hay House, 2004.

Chapter Four

Hawkins, David R. *Power vs. Force: The Hidden Determinants of Human Behavior.* Carlsbad, CA: Hay House, 2002.

Chapter Five

Burnham, Sophy. *Book of Angels: Reflections on Angels Past and Present, and True Stories of How They Touch Our Lives.* New York: Random House Publishing Group, 2004.

Ferrini, Paul. *Love Without Condition (Reflection of The Christ Mind Series), Vol. 1.* Greenfield, MA: Heartways Press, 1994.

Price, John Randolph. *The Angels Within Us.* New York: Random House Group Publishing, 1993.

Roman, Sanaya. *Soul Love: Awakening Your Heart Centers, Vol. 1.* Tiburon, CA: Starseed Press, 1997.

Chapter Six

Holmes, Ernest. *The Science of Mind.* New York: Penguin Group (USA), 1998.

Ruiz, Don Miguel. *The Four Agreements: A Practical Guide to Personal Freedom.* Carlsbad, CA: Hay House, 1997.

Roman, Sanaya. *Living With Joy: Keys to Personal Power and Spiritual Transformation*. Tiburon, CA: Starseed Press, 1986.

Chapter Seven

Dwoskin, Hale. *The Sedona Method: Your Key to Lasting, Happiness, Success, Peace And Emotional Well-Being*. Sedona, AZ: Sedona Press, 2003.

Hay, Louise L. *You Can Heal Your Life*. Carlsbad, CA: Hay House, 1984.

Tipping, Colin C. *Radical Forgiveness: Making Room for the Miracle*. Northboro, MA: Quest Publishing and Distribution, 2002.

Chapter Eight

Dyer, Wayne W. *Change Your Thoughts - Change Your Life: Living the Wisdom of the Tao*. Carlsbad, CA: Hay House, 2007.

Chopra, Deepak. *Power, Freedom, and Grace: Living from the Source of Lasting Happiness*. San Rafael. CA: Amber-Allen Publishing, 2006.

--- *The Seven Spiritual Laws of Success: A Practical Guide to the Fulfillment of Your Dreams*. San Rafael. CA: Amber-Allen Publishing, 1995.

Collins, Terah Kathryn. *The Western Guide to Feng Shui: Creating Balance, Harmony, and Prosperity in Your Environment*. Carlsbad, CA: Hay House, 1996.

Hill, Napoleon. *Think and Grow Rich*. New York: Random House Publishing Group, 1987.

Price, John Randolph. *The Abundance Book*. Carlsbad, CA: Hay House, 1996.

Roman, Sanaya. *Creating Money: Attracting Abundance*. Tiburon, CA: H. J. Kramer, 2007.

Shinn, Florence Scovel. *The Game of Life and how to Play It*. Marina del Rey, CA: DeVorss Publications, 1979.

Chapter Nine

Dass, Ram. *Be Here Now*. New York: Crown Publishing Group, 1971.

Peck, M. Scott. *The Road Less Traveled*. New York: Simon and Schuster, 1978.

Stovall, Jim. *The Ultimate Gift*. Mechanicsburg, PA: Executive Books, 2000.

Schwartz, Robert. *Courageous Souls: Do We Plan Our Life Challenges before Birth?* Cleveland, OH: Whispering Winds Press, 2007.
--- *Your Soul's Plan: Discovering the Real Meaning of the Life You Planned Before You Were Born*. New York: Random House, 2009. New Edition.

About The Author

A Metaphysical Teacher on Spirituality and life long practitioner of meditation, Robert Pease was born in the United States and educated on three continents. After an emotionally turbulent childhood, he began reading and studying philosophy and spirituality longing to discover and explore the inner journey of the Self. At nineteen he began practicing meditation and by twenty-two was living in Japan working for the U.S. Navy Department of Special Services. While in Japan he directed musicals, taught theater arts and co-created a Japanese award winning children's summer program for which he received the Good Fellowship Commendation from the government of Japan. After four years he moved to Hawaii and received a scholarship to study Japanese Kabuki Theater Arts at The University of Hawaii East West Center. Later he returned to the mainland to live in San Francisco to study further spiritual practices. Always the adventurer, having traveled and studied in India, China, Nepal, and South East Asia, he moved to Italy to continue to teach and study spirituality and fine arts. It was here that he was involved in a catastrophic automobile accident which took the lives of two friends. He had a personal near death experience which left him in hospital isolation for nearly one year. After an intense personal recovery including drug rehabilitation from pain inhibitors, he returned to America during the explosion of AIDS in the world. Providing care and companionship for many, many friends, he became connected to the work of Louise Hay and her deep commitment to living a positive affirmed life. Driven by her work, he began to acknowledge within himself his psychic intuitive ability which had been kept hidden since childhood. Growing up gay and psychic was not popular in his hometown in 1950's America. Compelled to move to New

York City, he continued to study and teach spirituality. He worked in the film, television and theater industry for over a decade while coaching actors and celebrities alike. Always passionate about the performing and designing arts, he became involved in co-producing and co-designing the off-Broadway hit "Boobs! The Musical" in 2000. While working on the television show "Third Watch," he was once again affected by the catastrophic event on September 11, 2001 when the loss of several friends and colleagues changed how he would view his life's journey and plan. After several years of living and loving New York City, he and his domestic partner of sixteen years moved to the desert sands of Arizona to begin teaching and writing full time, committed to the inner journey of the heart.

The journey continues in his development as a Reiki Master, an ordained minister, seminar leader, psychic and a spiritual mentor for businesses as well as individuals. He is completing his Ph.D. in 2009 in metaphysical research and developing programs, courses, and workshops as CEO of Robert Pease International. He is currently in production of an Internet variety show on spirituality to launch in 2009.

www.ingramcontent.com/pod-product-compliance
Lightning Source LLC
Chambersburg PA
CBHW060004100426
42740CB00010B/1390